SHORT CUTS

Copyright October 2018

By Oscar the Barber

Dedication

This book is dedicated to my mom, Seyhan Taskin. She has pancreatic cancer and two years later she is still alive and fighting it like she fought to raise me. Cancer sucks! Thank you, Mom.

SHORT CUTS

OSCAR THE BARBER

REMARKS:

"A Must Read about Life, Reality and Hard Work"! Don't miss the subtle humor integrated with "Life Lessons" "Oscar the Barber" perfectly cuts throughout it all"! This story should be an entertaining and insightful Documentary!

Steve Kalafer

OTB (Oscar The Barber) has been cutting my hair for over 20 years. Every appointment was not just a haircut. It was an adventure, an event, a great interaction of swapping stories, sharing human values and principles, DIY recommendations, nurturing a dialogue of unique situations and experiences while in his chair. This book and each chapter is vivid example of our time in the chair. However, more importantly Oscar and I share a mutual respect and a unique relationship somewhat similar to father and son. I immediately admired Oscar's positive can-do attitude, his enterprising mind, and his strong personal values the very first time I meet him. Hope you enjoy the book as getting to know Oscar is a treat.

Wayne Grimm

In a lifetime of haircuts I've never known a
barber as good as Oscar. He's fun to talk to,
too. But I have to be careful. I might wind up
in a book."

Don Crinklaw

I've sat in Oscar's chair every two weeks
for YEARS and know him to be a great barber
and my friend... after reading all of these
stories that tell it like it is, I know why I
am not included. His other customers are
FAR more interesting. Well done, my
friend!   **Allen Zeman**

This book is a FUN read! I had a hard
time putting it down. Oscar weaves great
short stories beautifully.   I could really see
and feel his clients! Hope Hollywood reads
this, would make a great T.V. series!! Nice job
my friend.

Maybin Grimm

Raw, real and captivating stories told
from the chair of Oscar the Barber!
Cristiana Pecheanu

Stories from the chair told by the best
Barber to stand behind the chair. Great job!!

Ralph S. Screnci

I have never met Oscar but I was
given the opportunity to read the book. I
laughed and cried. A must read!
Donna Simon

Acknowledgments

Wow. Finally, I turned an idea into a very cool collection of stories. I'd been gathering these stories in my mind, but soon I realized that I needed help, professional help, to make them into a book.

I waited to see my dear client, Don Crinklaw, in my chair. He was one of the first reporters who broke the story about me in a newspaper. He was so excited to hear about my project and this is when I heard Elaine Viets' name. She's his wife! Luck is where hard work meets preparation.

Elaine has written and published 33 mysteries. The book business is what she does. This book would not be the way it is without her guidance and mentorship. I really appreciate her efforts.

I want to thank Helene Unstad for being there with me. She was the first one who loved the stories and she has great intuition. I appreciate her calm, care and love.

I also want to thank Cristiana Pecheanu for the cover photo and Donna Simon for the amazing design of the cover of the book.

I want to thank all my clients, whether or not they're in this book, for allowing me to have fun while I work. I feel so lucky to have the clients I have.
I've changed all the customers' names and some details, but all these stories are real.

I also want to thank my coworkers for putting up with me and my stories.

Most importantly, I want to thank my mom, Seyhan Taskin. She was diagnosed with pancreatic cancer two years ago and she is still alive and fighting it. She used that same spirit to fight to raise me. Again, thank you, Mom!

Table of Contents

Introducing Oscar the Barber	1
The Man with the Wife No Man Could See	8
The Reason to Live	15
The Porn Stars	18
The Rock 'n Roll Cruise	24
The Will	28
The Last Wish	29
Billie the New Yorker	31
The Enterprising Twins	35
The Cool Jacket	38
The Important Man	39
Independent Day	47
Investing in Sexy Pictures	53
Judging a Book by Its Cover	57
The Cool Father and Son	61
The Funky Lady	64
The Merry Christmas	67
The Billionaire	69
The Woman with the Shaved Head	71
The Good Husband	75
The Shelby Mustang	79

The Revenge of the Rich Girl 84

The Man with One Eyebrow 88

The Harley-Davidson 91

The Woman Who Would Not Dye 99

The Tough Guy 104

The Martini Friendship 108

The Man Nobody Knew 112

The Man Who Had One Beer 119

The Macho Man 123

The Sick Man 128

The Famous Chef 132

The Hollywood Big Deal 135

The Philly Cheese Steak 138

The Man with Four Daughters 143

The Treasure Hunter 146

The US Marshal 150

The Crooked Lawyer 155

The Millionaire Who Met Madoff 159

The Man with Someone Else's Lungs 167

The Man with the Bag of Money 169

The Free Advice 174

The Dead Man's Hair 179

The Good Example 184

The Famous Athlete 185

The Man Who Found a New Reason to Live 192

The Abused Man   197

The Man Who Sexted   201

The Man Who Wanted Short Hair   204

The Light at the End of the Tunnel   209

A New Start from a Stranger   213

The Man Who Told Wild Stories   215

The Man Who Lost 20 Years   217

Barry and the Blind Man   220

Eddie and the Strip Club CD   224

Mike the Gangster   228

Dino's Heart   232

Photo of Oscar and his Barber Tools   236

Contact Information for Oscar the Barber   237

Notes Page   238

Introducing Oscar the Barber

I'm from Istanbul, Turkey. I have a computer background and a degree in psychology. I started working in a salon here in the United States. I thought cutting hair looked interesting. A couple of good friends pushed me to go to school and get my license. They said, "You're good with people. You'll make a great barber." I started cutting hair part-time and now it's my profession. At first, it was a way of making money, but I fell in love with my customers and their stories.

I'm not an artist, like some hairstylists. I rely on technique for repeated results. What separates me from other barbers is I really care about my customers. If a regular says he's going in for tests, I make a note to call him. If I've heard someone's in the hospital, I check on him. But mostly, I listen.

Hundreds of people cut hair in this area. There are lots of barbers within two blocks. Some are more expensive, some are less. So why go to me?

When I was learning, I was told

a small part of the business of
barbering requires natural talent. Time
will sharpen that talent, but if you
don't like people, time will wear you
down. My fascination

with people and their stories has
really connected me to my profession.

In addition to listening, I give
my customers something special. The
men get an old school complimentary
neck shave with a straight razor. In
the US, most barbers quit using a
straight razor or they don't have the
education to use it. Training in the
barbering industry is becoming very
industrial. Most barbershops and
barbers are like factories, cutting hair
and calling "Next"! Real barbers like
myself are decreasing by the day. I
treat my customers like they're my
friends and I want them to feel that
way – like they can call me to have
drinks or dinner with them. Respect is
one thing that develops out of caring
and friendship. I provide that to all
my clients and expect the same from
them. It's not really hard to have long-
lasting relationships if you are
genuine with people.

Barbers are like pianists – we all
have our style. I want to know a client.

That's my style. When a new client
makes an appointment, I make sure I
have a few extra minutes. Then I go
outside and meet him. I get to see
what he drives, what he's wearing,
how he walks. I personally welcome
him to my shop and help him off with
his jacket. I never judge anyone
during my initial observation.
However, I take mental notes to make
my new client feel more comfortable.
We have something to talk about if he
is wearing a hat with a feather, or
driving a fast sports car. Maybe he just
likes the wind to blow through his
long hair.

 Then we talk for a bit. I ask a lot
of questions: Where does he live?
What does he do for a living? Does he
use hair products? I want to build a
long-term relationship with him.

 If you say to me, "I'm a pilot," on
your first visit, I'll tell you, "Some of
my clients are pilots. Do you fly
commercial or private?"

 If he says "private," I'll say,
"Single engine? Double? The G-7
series?"

 He'll say, "You know something
about planes."

 I'll say, "You wear a collared

shirt. Do you want your hair short?"

Usually he – and sometimes she – will say, "Short, but not too short. I don't want a crewcut."

The relationships I have with my clients didn't develop overnight. They take time. It helps if my customers are a little early for their appointments. If they're going to be late, they should tell me. Otherwise, if someone is ten minutes late, then I can't wait on the next customer on time and soon the whole day is off. I want to deliver the expected service with the same quality every time. If you're late to an appointment, that takes away from everyone's quality that day. I am a perfectionist.

I read, watch, and try to inform myself as much as possible daily. Especially when I have a new client with an interest or a job that I'm not familiar with. I want to learn about his interests before the next cut. It's always better to have a chat with collected information.

I keep asking questions until my new customers feel comfortable. Then they say something like, "Go ahead. I trust you."

I'll say, "Don't trust me yet. Let's

see the haircut first."

After I know my clients, I know what they want to do when they get their hair cut. Some want to talk about their marriage. That's fine. Others talk about business. Some business types say, "I don't want any bullshit talk. Just give me a haircut." That's fine, too.

I can tell by looking at you who cut your hair. I can look at someone's hair and say, "Your regular barber is an old school Italian. He's in his 60s or 70s." Or I'll tell them, "You get your hair cut by a woman. She's very hot. She takes 40 minutes to cut your hair and uses ten different scissors."

The clients always say, "How did you know?"

I know hair the way other people know art.

I've had guys who go to women stylists because these stylists were good-looking. Somehow, these men all find their way back to my chair. I know talented female hair stylists and very good-looking ones. However, if the stylist is chosen because of her great-looking boobs, she's not going to give you a good haircut.

Getting your hair cut is an

intimate service. You're trying to explain what you want, but you don't know how to describe it. Show me a picture and ask me if that style is right for you. I'll tell you. Most importantly, don't tell me how to do my job! I don't ask the butcher how to cut the filet. I ask him for a lean filet. Let me do what I do every day.

If a man comes in with snow-white hair and wants to dye it coal-black, I won't do it. I know it's going to look bad. I don't want his wife telling him his hair sucks and then have him say, "Oscar the Barber did that." It goes back to building that long-term relationship.

Once you're a regular, I'm like a bartender. I'll remember how you want your hair cut.

My clients tend to be older, richer, and successful. Older people are more stable, more loyal, and more likely to show up on time. Many own their own businesses. I'd say 70% of my clients are 50 and older, and the other 30% are their sons and wives. I cut mostly men's hair. South Florida has cool people – lots of Canadians and East Coasters come down during the season – from November to

Passover or Easter.

I have been talking with my clients about putting some of my stories in a book for a while. One of them said, "Wow, you are shooting for the moon."

Here's the good thing about shooting for the moon: Even if you miss the moon, you will hit something high up there. I always aim high! I take pride and respect myself and the people around me.

I've cut thousands of heads over the years. **I've changed the names and some of the circumstances to protect my clients.** Here are some of the stories I have heard. **Oscar the Barber November, 2018**

The Man with the Wife No Man Could See

This customer tells me, "This guy from New York, he needs a good barber."

I say, "Okay, send him to me."

"He's a bit of an eccentric guy, so just play along with him," my customer says. "His name is Ray."

So Ray calls me and says, "Kid, let me tell you something, when I come in, I don't want anyone in the shop."

I say, "Well, sir, I can't guarantee that."

He says, "How many chairs do you have in the shop?"

I say, "Three."

He says, "I'll pay for everyone's haircuts, so you don't lose money, but I want the shop empty."

I say, "Sir, I can't promise that, but how about if you come on a Wednesday as my last customer? I'll make sure everyone clears out."

He says, "Perfect."

So he comes in on a Wednesday around three-thirty. The place is empty. I see this black Town Car pull up. These two guys come out of there, both in black suits, looking like they belong in that car and I'm thinking, Is this the guy? It's the time for his appointment.

So he gets out of the car, and he's this big heavy dude and he's got this belt and he just pulls it up. He's not an old guy – he's maybe late thirties, but he acts like he's seventy years old. So he walks toward my shop and the two guys come in first and one says, "Are you Oscar?" and I say I was and he wanted to look inside.

I thought he was going to use the restroom or something. So he goes around the shop, goes back out, tells the other guy, "It's okay."

Ray comes, it's like this big deal. The two guys open the door and in he comes. One of the black suits stays on one side of the door, the other suit stays on the other side.

"You Oscar?" Ray asks. I say I am. "Nobody in the shop?"

"Nobody," I say.

"Which one is your station?" he asks.

"This one." So he comes and sits down. He had a beautiful suit, but he was sweating and he had one of those towels to mop up the sweat. Very

Italian. Very macho.

"You know how to shave?" he asks.

I say, "Yeah, I been doing it for a long time."

He says, "Give me a shave and a haircut."

I do a shave and a haircut. He doesn't say a word. He had me so intimidated, I got him in and out of there quick.

At the end, he gives me a large bill and gives me a really good tip. He says, "I want to come every week, same time, same place, same accommodations."

So this continued – second time, third time, fourth time, fifth time. Every week. We went about three months like that. So it's coming to the beginning of the season and I'm thinking, Now in the season, it's going to be hard to keep the shop open like this – with no one coming late Wednesday afternoon.

I'd become very friendly with him, so I thought maybe he could change his hours and come in earlier or later. So we talk about it, I get his points, he gets mine.

I'd become very friendly with

him, so I thought maybe he could change his hours and come in earlier or later. So we talk about it, I get his points, he gets mine. He says to me, "Oscar, next time, I want to bring my wife in with me. But I have to tell you, you can't look at my wife."

I'm thinking, Ooookay.

He says, "I'm telling you, I don't want you looking at her, checking her out, none of that stuff."

He says to one of the two suits, "Tell him what happened to the last guy who looked at my wife."

"We had to take care of some business," the suit says.

I don't know what that means.

Ray says, "I like you. I been coming here once a week. You're a cool kid. Let's not break this."

I say, "Okay, no problem."

Before he leaves he says, "I'm telling you one more time, I don't want you looking at her."

Now the question pops into my mind, What the hell's going on? Why's he even bringing his wife in the shop? She's not getting her hair done. She's just coming to watch him get a haircut and shave.

Now I wanna look at her. I keep

running all these scenarios through my mind: Is she gonna come in the front door? If I do see her will he come out of the chair and get pissed at me? I don't know what's going on, but I'm nervous.

The nervousness is building up, so on the next Wednesday, here comes the car. I couldn't not look at the car. It's pulling up in front of my place. Ray gets out by himself and I think, Oh, great, the wife is not coming.

As soon as he comes in, he points his finger at me and says, "Oscar, my wife is coming in soon and I told you, don't do nothing to ruin our relationship."

I'm like, "No problem, man. Just chill. I'm not going to look at her." So there's one suit outside the door and one suit inside of the door and I cut Ray's hair and I lay him down in the chair for his shave. That's how we do the shaves, I lay the men down and lather them up and then I put this hot towel on their face. So as I'm Lathering him up, with this hot towel next to me, and I hear the chime of the door. Here she comes in. I'm like, Oscar, don't look at her. Oscar, don't look at her. I have the mirror in front of me, and she sits right where I can see her in the mirror. It's impossible NOT to see her.

Here I am trying to lather up his face and oh my God, she walks in with those stilettos, she smells so good and I'm a man. I think, What the hell, I want a peek at her.

Is she a movie star? A super model? I have to know. Her perfume is all over the barber shop.

So I think, Screw it. When I put the towel on, I can have a little peek.

I'm lathering up his face. He's calm. His eyes are closed. I look at the other two suits, they're doing their thing, looking outside, so I take that hot towel and I push it on his face and I make sure I push that eye section so he's not watching through the towel.

And I look and I peek out of the corner of my eye and there she is, a beautiful, blonde gorgeous woman. Young. Maybe thirty. She is tall and dressed up – wow! When she walked in the room, it was a statement. She could walk in any place and every guy would turn around and look at her.

And as soon as I look, she looks back at me. She knew I looked and I shouldn't have.

Ray takes the towel off his face and throws it on the floor and says, "Get me up! Get me up!"

Now the woman just walks out of the door.

He says to me, "Kid! The fuck did I tell you? Did I tell you not to look at my wife? I'm asking you: Did I or not?"

I say, "Yes, you did."

"Did I say, Don't even peek at her?"

"Yes, you did."

"Did I tell you I didn't want to ruin a good relationship and I wouldn't like it here if you did that?"

"Yes, you did."

"But what you did – tell me what you did? You put the towel on my face and you peeked at my wife, didn't you?"

I say, "Yes, I did."

He says, "Why?"

I say, "I don't know. I don't know why."

He says, "You should never ruin a good relationship. Cancel all my appointments."

He walked out and I've never heard from him again. A man will always be a man.

The Reason to Live

Frederick's been coming to me for a long time. He's one of those old New Jersey-New York wise guys. But he's a smooth guy. He's the type of wise guy who's like Robert De Niro in *Casino,* right? You look at this guy and you know he has something. He dresses well, he owns nightclubs. He comes to me one day and he doesn't look well. And I say, "Hey, Frederick, what's wrong? You look like you're not feeling well."

And he says, "Well, I've got this prostate problem."

I say, "Yeah, I know, I can see you been going through something bad."

As I'm talking to him, he gets agitated. He says, "I know, and it's been giving me a hard time. You know what, Oscar, they removed it."

I say, "Oh, wow. Was it difficult?"

He says, "No, it was like an emergency thing. They thought the treatment was going to work out, but the cancer was so bad the doctor said they had to remove it. At first, I didn't think anything about it, but the doctor says, 'You might have some complications sexually.'" And I say, "What do you mean?"

And Frederick says, "What do you mean?" Now he was really excited. "It's OVER! The game is over!"

"What do you mean?"

"Nothing happens. When you don't have your prostate, nothing goddamn happens!" He's really upset, really agitated.

I say, "Frederick, take it easy."

He says, "Don't tell me to take it easy! Everybody God dammit tells me to take it easy! You know what, Oscar?"

"What?"

He takes his gun out of his belt and puts it right underneath his chin. I'm thinking, Oh, my God! He's freaking out! He's going to shoot himself.

He says to me, "You know how many times I get so close I just want to pull this trigger? You know what keeps me going? **YOU KNOW WHAT KEEPS ME GOING?**"

I'm thinking, What the fuck! Put the gun away!

He says, "Golf!"

He says, "I got to be honest. I got into golf. I have absolutely no pressure any more. I go to the golf course, I forget all about it."

He put the gun away. I'm thinking, Jesus, you just gave me a heart attack.

The Porn Stars

It's an off-season summer day, the shop is quiet, and I'm about to walk out. I've just switched the sign to CLOSED and this guy, Rick, is on the other side of the door. The lights are off and he's knocking on the door.

I'm like, "Dude, we're closed."

Rick says, "Come on, one more, one more. I wanna get a haircut."

I'm like, "Dude, I'm telling you, I'm closing. I want to go home. I got plans."

He's on the other side, we're talking through the door. He takes a hundred bucks, he puts it on the glass so it's flat and he says, "One cut, a hundred bucks."

I'm like, "Okay." It's a hundred bucks. He doesn't have much hair – he could have gone to Supercuts. It's going to take me like ten minutes. But no, he wanted me.

So he comes in and he says, "Thank you so much."

I say, "Dude, a hundred bucks is a lot of money for a haircut."

He says, "No, no, you were gonna leave. Look at this hair. You can't fuck this up."

So Rick sits in my chair, and I put the cape on him. We used to have a beach store down the street from us, and here's this good-looking girl who's been shopping there. She comes into my shop while I'm cutting Rick's hair and he says, "Oh, honey, this is Oscar. He's a super cool guy and he's going to cut my hair."

She says, "Oh, that's great." She's very attractive. She's wearing sandals and a miniskirt. A very short miniskirt. She's got large boobs. She looks hot – sexuality drips from her.

As I'm cutting Rick's hair she's sitting where I can see her in the mirror. She opens her legs. I'm looking, as a man, right? And she's looking at me, and I see her open her legs even more.

And I'm thinking, Whoa!

Then she pulls her skirt all the way up and I'm thinking, What the hell is going on here?

I'm getting nervous now.

So I'm trying not to pay attention to the woman and Rick says, "Hey, are you checking out my wife?"

I say, "No, I'm not looking at your wife."

He says, "Yes, you were." He

turned around and says to her, "Hey, Audi" – his next words were kind of shocking – "Hey, Audi, show him your pussy."

I'm like, "What!?"

He says, "It's okay, over like ten million people have seen it, so it doesn't make a difference if one more sees it."

I'm going, "Dude, you got me all wrong. I don't know what's going on here." My brain is not functioning fast enough to take this in. Are they swingers? Why is he cool with me looking at her? Is this a joke?

I say, "Here's your hundred bucks, you can go now."

He says, "No, no, finish the cut."

I say, "I want to, but I'm getting very uncomfortable with you. And your wife is getting naked."

He says, "Oscar, we are both in the adult industry."

I say, "So what's that mean?"

"We make porno movies. We're porn stars. You've never seen my wife? You're a young guy."

Back then there was no internet. Movies were VHS tapes.

I say, "I don't know, man. I don't know."

Rick says, "I'll show you some brochures and stuff. Audi, go get some brochures from the car."

She gets the brochures and posters of herself naked and she signs a poster and gives it to me. I'm like, This is awkward.

Rick says, "Listen, we are humans. All we do is adult movies. We all do it. *We* just do it for other people on camera."

I say, "I never met anybody like you guys. How long have you been together?"

He says, "Oh, we've been together for like twenty years."

I say, "Twenty years. How did you guys meet?"

He says, "In the adult industry. It's so hard to have a relationship in this industry."

I say, "Really? You don't have a problem that your wife is having sex with other men on camera and everybody's watching it?"

He says, "Nope, it's like going to work. She does her job well, and we watch it together."

I'm like, "Really?"

He says, "We even have two kids."

I say, "Really?"

He says, "They live with their grandparents while we're off shooting movies. We're no different than any ordinary family. We watch TV at night, and stuff like that."

I'm like, Whoa! This is mind-blowing.

He says to me, "You really don't know who you're talking to. You've never seen us in action."

I'm thinking, What are they going to do? Do it in the shop?

He says, "This would be a great scene. We could shoot a movie in the shop."

I say, "Absolutely NOT!"

He says, "Why? You have something against porn stars?"

I say, "I have nothing against you guys. I gotta think about this."

He says, "How about if I send you a couple of cassettes? You watch us, and if you want, we'll come and shoot a movie here."

I say, "All right." He takes one of my business cards and they left.

I thought, Oh my God, what a weird situation to be in. I didn't think about them again until a month later, when the mail is delivered to the shop. It's a Saturday, and the shop is full. I've got this mailing tube and a box, and I think, What is this? Sometimes I get beauty product posters.

I open up the poster. In front of everyone. Guess who was in it?

Audi – absolutely naked. And a couple of cassettes. "We love you, Oscar," is all over the stuff.

The Rock 'n Roll Cruise

It always seems like the good stories happen at the end of the day. I was working in a hair salon, and I was just doing barbering. The other stylists in the front of the shop cut women's hair. I see this beautiful woman come in with her girlfriend. She was a redhead, she had red hair down to her waist.

She says to me, "Excuse me, can I get a haircut?"

I say, "I'm sorry, I don't do ladies' haircuts. I'm a barber. You're going to have to go in the front, where there are ten hairdressers."

She says to me, "No, no, I specifically want you to do my haircut."

I say, "I'll try, but the stylists up front do what they do best."

She says, "No, no, I want a funky haircut. I want to cut it all off."

I say, "Cut it all off? You have beautiful, gorgeous red hair." She'd recently colored it a deep red, like a punk red. "Why would you want to cut that hair? You hate the color, then change the color."

She says, "If you give me a

haircut I'll tell you why."

I say, "Then sit down." I was curious about why she was doing it.

As soon as she sits down, she says to me, "I've got breast cancer."

I say, "Oh, I'm so sorry to hear that."

She says, "That's okay. This is my fourth time."

Again, I said I was sorry.

She says, "There's no going back. This is it. The doctors did the best they could. I'm so tired. I don't want to fight any more."

She was like in her thirties, a young girl. I was really sorry to hear that.

She says, "I've always want to go on this rock cruise, with all these rock bands. My best friend says, 'Let's do it. It will be good for you.' I've lived my whole life as a conservative person. I've always done what I'm supposed to do. So what the hell, my life is pretty short. I'm gonna take chances and do what I want to do."

So I say, "What do you want to do?"

She says, "Make me look like a punk rocker."

I say, "Well, you got the hair

color. What we could do is a badass Mohawk."

She says, "Exactly what I need."

I say, "I was just kidding. I could chop your hair off and make it look punky."

She says, "No, I want a Mohawk."

I say, "A Mohawk *Mohawk*, like a real Mohawk?"

She says, "Exactly. Shave the sides of my head completely. And leave the middle very long."

I say, "Wow, that's gonna be a transformation!"

She says, "That's what I want. Can you do that?"

Now it's happened before in my career that people ask for dramatic changes. I've learned that when people go through emotional stuff the first thing they want to do is cut their hair. Change their appearance. It's not always a good idea.

I was gonna tell her no. It was too drastic. But she told me she'd had breast cancer four times, she's gonna die, she's so young, and this is one thing she wants to experience, so I say, "You know what? Let's do it."

So I worked on her and I gave

her a beautiful Mohawk. She looked like a punk rocker. When we finished, she looked at herself and she was crying. I don't know if she was crying because she had cancer, because finally for the first time she did something she really wanted to do, but now it's just too late. Maybe she wanted to do a lot of other different things but she was out of time.

She says, "Thank you," and left with her friend.

Life is short. As one of my late clients told me, "Don't postpone joy."

The Will

The other day, my customer says he just made his will. I say, "Did you put my name in there?"

He says, "Oscar, I love you, but not that much."

I say, "Think about it. I've been cutting your hair for a long time: Every time you have a wedding. Every time you have a bar mitzvah. Every time you have a funeral. Every time you get a job interview. When you get together with your friends. When you see your brother. When your kids come into town.

"Who's the first person you call? Oscar. And you go get a haircut. So I've been with you for all these memorable moments. I am the guy behind the scenes, making it all happen. In all those good memories, maybe if you'd had a bad haircut, it would have ruined one of them.

"And your ears. How many people touch your ears? Your wife, your kids and me. We're more intimate than you realize."

The Last Wish

Another busy day. I'm in this new shop and it's packed, right? I'm trying to do my customers and sometimes people come in without an appointment. This woman comes in and she says, "I just need a haircut."

This is a typical thing when people come in and say, "Just a haircut" like I can do it in a minute, right?

I say, "We are very busy. How about tomorrow or the next day?"

She says, "No! I really need a haircut right now."

I say, "I can't do it right now. What am I supposed to do?" I'm not arguing with her, and she's not being nasty to me, but she's very insistent.

She says, "I need a haircut today because today is the day I feel like cutting my hair off."

I say, "Okay, but why can't you come tomorrow?"

She says, "My husband is dying from pancreatic cancer. And he's always asked me to cut my hair short. I've always said, 'No! I don't want to cut my hair. What are you, crazy? I'll look like a boy.' And today he says to

me, 'It's still not too late. I still want to
see you with short hair.'"

"I say, "Lady, I'm gonna tell you
something and you won't believe it.
My mom has pancreatic cancer."
(Thank God, she's still alive.) I say to
the haircut lady, "That is going to get
you in the door today. Because your
husband has pancreatic cancer. Not
because I'm feeling bad about you and
you husband. Because I know exactly
what you guys are going through,
because of my mom. Let's do the cut."

So for the first time in my career,
I actually made another customer wait
half an hour. I told them I was
running late and I cut her hair.

She loved it, the husband loved
it.

He died and she moved on and
married someone else, but she stayed
in touch with her first husband's
family. Sometimes, the coincidences in
life bring people together. She is still a
client.

Billie the New Yorker

Billie is one of those old school New Yorkers – he says, "Let me tell you something." Every time he comes in he hugs me and touches my chest.

I say, "Dude, why're you touching my chest?" and he says, "I just wanna make sure I know you and nobody's wired."

So this became a big joke. Every time he came in the shop, he'd check for a wire.

Billie had almost no hair. He barely had a few strands on top – maybe like twenty-thirty strands – and it's not very thick on the sides. He used to come in to the shop four times a week. One day, he says, "Hey, can I ask you a question?"

I say, "Yeah. What is it?"

He says, "You do blow dries?"

I say, "Yeah, you want a blow dry?" He doesn't have that much hair.

He says, "Yeah, I'll start coming in every day. What do you charge for a blow dry?"

I give him a price and he says, "Good. I'll start coming every day."

He was such a nervous guy. He was worried I was wired and I could

never call him on the phone. I'd call
him up and I'd say like, "Hey, Billie."
He'd never answer. He was like silent.
I'd say, "Are you coming today?"

He didn't want to answer. So we
figured it out. We'd use numbers. If
he'd press one if it was yes, if he
pressed three, the answer was no. I
could tell by the tone. Sometimes I
used to fuck with him and say, "Did
you press three or one?"

He'd yell into the phone, "God
damn it, how many times did I tell
you? One sounds different than three.
I'm coming today, dammit. How
many times did I tell you? I don't
want to talk on the phone. There's
rats."

He even bought a Cadillac and
got the GPS removed. The dealer told
him, "Billie, it comes with the car."
Billie says, "I want it removed. I don't
want everybody to know my
business."

I always had a baseball bat next
to my station. Protection, or it looked
good in a barber shop, I don't know.
One morning, Billie says to me, "Hey,
Oscar, can I borrow the bat for a
while?"

I say, "Yeah. What are you gonna

do with the bat?"

He says, "I'm gonna take care of some business."

He's not going to take care of anything. He just wants the baseball bat. I know.

I say, "Look, don't walk around with that baseball bat. You're gonna get in trouble."

He says, "Oh, yeah? What kinda trouble?"

I say, "I know people. You know people. It's not a good idea."

I'm just messing with him. We go outside in the parking lot. He's got this baseball bat and he says, "Come on, come on. I'm an old man but I can still hit hard."

He's just messing around. The next thing you know, these four cops are coming out of their cars. I mean, they are charging us. And I'm like, "No, no! This is a joke!"

They pinned Billie to a car. One has handcuffs, one is yelling at him. I'm yelling, "Dudes, no! Stop!"

They're looking at me. One cop says, "Why?"

I say, "Because he's just messing with me. We were joking around."

The cops start apologizing, but

Billie, he's not happy. Here he is, this tough guy pinned to a car.

He says to me, "Hey, Oscar, the whole time I was playing!"

Once a player, a player for life.

The Enterprising Twins

I had these twins who used to come to me. They looked so much alike even I couldn't tell them apart. Their hairlines were the same, everything. They're good-looking guys with piercing blue eyes, blondish hair. They were like super cool guys. They worked out and had a lot of muscle. They were striking, both of them.

When I was working in the hair salon, and they would come in, the girls were like, "Oh, my God. Which one is which?"

I really didn't know.

They were giving me big tips, driving big cars. They didn't strike me as educated, professional dudes, they struck me as hustlers.

I realized some days they were twitching a little bit. One day I asked, "What do you guys do for a living?"

They told me they owned a bunch of pain clinics. This was before the state closed them down. I say, "Well, that's interesting. How many do you guys own?"

They owned like several of them.

They came to me for a year.

They never talked about business or anything like that. One day I'm home, watching TV. My girlfriend says to me, "Oscar, is that one of the cute guys who comes to your shop?"

I look at the TV, and there's a guy being arrested, and it's him! One of the twins! Oh my God! They got busted!

The state was busting the pain clinics. Now they're looking for the other twin.

I'm thinking, what if the police come here and ask me questions? I don't know anything about it. I just cut their hair.

I'm thinking this is so sad. Should I call them? What if their phones are being tapped?

Three days later, one of the twins shows up. The guy on TV is in my shop. I'm like, "Dude, what are you doing in here?"

He says, "Oscar, did you see what happened? Do you know?"

I say, "The whole town knows. The cops are looking for you. You have to turn yourself in. Are you guys crazy?"

He says, "No, man. Hold on! My brother and I were together. I don't

know what happened. I guess one of
the doctors was doing something
illegal. My brother got busted. I was
home. I escaped. I didn't know what
to do."

I say, "What are you doing in
here?"

"I'm going to turn myself in," he
says. "And I thought about it at home.
I thought, at least I'll get one more
good haircut before I go to jail."

I say, "Are you serious?"

He says, "Yeah. Can you cut my
hair? I'm going to jail right after I
leave here."

I cut his hair and I say, "Was it
worth it, what you did?"

He says, "Yes. We come from a
very poor family. We always dreamed
of a big life and we thought it would
be so hard to achieve it. My brother
and I said, 'Fuck it, let's do it.'
Hopefully, it's going to blow over and
we'll get out of jail."

I cut his hair and he left. Both
went to jail.

The Cool Jacket

I go to this nice, fancy restaurant and I had this jacket with a cool dragon embedded in the back of it. Several of my customers work in this restaurant and one, Charlie, comes up to me and says, "Dude, I'm digging the jacket. It's awesome."

I say, "Thank you."

A couple more times during my meal he'd say, "I love that jacket. I love that jacket."

He comes for a haircut and he says he has something special going on in upstate New York and he says, "I don't have a jacket."

I say, "Considering you don't have a jacket" – he's been living in Florida a long time – "how about you take my jacket? The dragon jacket. The one you like."

He says, "Are you serious?"

I say, "Sure. It's just a jacket. You wear it. You'll bring it back, right?"

He says, "Oh, I'll make sure I dry-clean it. Nothing will happen to it."

I say, "I'm sure nothing's going to happen. It's just a jacket. You wear it a couple of hours, you return it. If something happens, it happens. Come tomorrow and I'll bring the jacket to work. If you can't get it dry-cleaned, don't worry about it. I know a good cleaner."

He takes the jacket. A month goes by. Six weeks go by. Now we're into three months and no jacket and I'm thinking, Where's my jacket? I'm also thinking, he's going to come in for a haircut. Maybe he didn't make it back down here to Florida. Maybe something happened.

So I go to the restaurant again, with a different jacket. And I see Charlie from afar, and he's not making eye contact with me. He's avoiding me. Also, he's not coming for haircuts any more.

I think, Hold on a second. I lend him a jacket and now he's not talking to me? Something happened to the jacket.

I try to catch his attention and he avoids me. When I'm ready to leave the place I say, "Hey, Charlie."

He says, "Hey, Oscar, my friend! How are you doing?"

I say, "I haven't seen you for a while."

"Oh," he says, "I'm so busy. My

shift changed. Your schedule is not good with my schedule."

I can see he got a haircut somewhere else. I don't want to make him feel bad.

"I had to go somewhere else," he says. "The new barber's nothing like you. I should have texted you."

I say, "Dude, no problem. You don't want to come to me for any reason, that's okay. But one thing. Where's my jacket? You lost it? Something happen to it? You can tell me."

He says, "No. I just didn't have time to call you."

I say, "*Three months*, Charlie? You went away for two days."

He says, "I promise I'll bring the jacket to you."

So a week later, I've been calling him every day and leaving messages: "Charlie, don't forget to bring my jacket."

Now it was more than the jacket. I thought I'd done something really good. I'd loaned him the jacket. Now he stops being a customer and doesn't return my phone calls.

So he finally brings the jacket and takes it out of the bag. "Look!

There's nothing wrong with the jacket, man. Stop bothering me."

I'm like, "Excuse me? I'm bothering *you*? It's my jacket."

He takes the jacket and puts it on himself and says, "Look, there's nothing wrong with the jacket."

And I look at it. I wear an extra-large and this guy wears a medium and I'm thinking, How does that jacket fit this dude so well?

I say, "Charlie, why does my jacket fit you so well?"

He says, "Oh, I had it fitted."

I say, "Charlie, you took my jacket to a tailor and you got it fitted on you?"

He says, "Yeah. How else could I wear it?"

I say, "It's my jacket! Didn't you think, before you got it fitted for yourself, 'How is Oscar going to wear this jacket?'"

He says, "Oh, man, you are right. I never thought of that. You think this jacket is not going to fit you?"

I say, "No! I couldn't even put my arm in the sleeve."

He says, "Oh, man, I never thought of that. You're a hundred percent right."

I say, "Charlie. Keep the jacket."

Now, at the shop, whenever I start to get mad, someone will say, "Hey, Oscar, can I borrow your jacket?" and I know I've been screwed with again.

The Important Man

I met this guy, Bill. He's very high up in Washington DC. He's a very, very powerful man in the government. You can tell when you meet a person like that: the way they talk, the way they present themselves, they're sharp. I knew immediately – this was somebody.

He has very little hair. We hit it off. He likes to talk about politics, not too much, just a little. He comes often. He's got a beautiful family. And he misses his appointment. I figure something went wrong at home.

I'm particular about appointments. Appointments are for a reason. If you have an appointment at nine a.m., I expect you to be there at nine a.m. Because that's how I make my money. You can't just walk in here at nine-thirty or ten o'clock when you've got a nine o'clock appointment.

I have a policy: Miss three appointments, and I stop cutting your hair. I send a nice text message that says, "Relationships have a shelf life. We've reached the end of that shelf life. Have a great day. All the best."

Bill comes in and says, "I missed

my appointment."

I say, "I know. You shouldn't do that. I'm losing money."

Second time, he doesn't show up. I give him a warning, "Bill, when we started this relationship, I told you, 'Three times no show, I've got to let you go. One more time, and that's it.'"

He says, "I promise, Oscar, I'm not going to miss another appointment."

I say, "Okay."

And he misses another appointment. That's three. So I send him the good-bye text message, "Relationships have a shelf life and we've just reach the end." And he keeps calling and calling. I realize someone in a powerful position, you can't just tell them no. They don't take no for an answer.

He comes into the shop on a busy day. He sits in a chair. I'm really uncomfortable. What's he going to say? Is he going to argue with me? Ask, Why don't you answer my phone calls? Should I say something? How is this going to end?

He comes to me and says, "Hey, Oscar, do you have a moment?"

"Yes, Bill."

He says, "Look, I'm gonna sit here until you give me another chance."

I say, "We had an agreement: three times and then we cut off the relationship. We agreed."

He says, "Here I am. Sitting. Apologizing to you in person. I have never done this for anyone else in my life. I realize other people's time is just as valuable as mine. I swear to God, it was something I shouldn't have done. I feel so bad. I feel terrible. I thought about it for two weeks: Should I go? Should I say something to Oscar? Then it hit me. Yes, I am the bigger man. I should have the guts to say something. I'm the one who missed the appointments."

He offered to pay for the three missed haircuts.

Here's what's going through my mind: This guy is in such a powerful position, but he has almost no hair. He's almost begging me to take him back. I'm not that good with hair cutting, but I'm good with relationships, with people. How can I say no? I didn't want his money. I wanted respect, and not showing up was a sign of disrespect.

I say, "Rules are made to be broken. Let's have a restart in our relationship."

And after that, he never missed another appointment. Ever. Invest in people.

Independent Day

"I started riding a motorcycle and I met a bunch of Israeli guys. They all started coming to me for haircuts. Israelis and Turkish people, they're very close culturally. I'm Muslim, but I grew up in a Jewish neighborhood in Istanbul, so I know how they think. I understand their attitude. So one of the guys, Avi, says, "Hey, Oscar, we're going for a motorcycle ride on Sunday. You wanna come?"

I say, "Yeah!"

Avi says, "There's gonna be a bunch of people, a bunch of people." He spoke broken English.

I say, "Who are these people?"

He says, "It's going to be a great Independent Day."

"Independent Day?"

He says, "Yeah, all your customers, all the guys who come to you, we're all gonna ride together and it's going to be a great Independent Day."

I say, "What do you mean, Independent Day?"

He says, "You know, *Independent* Day."

I say, "You mean Independence Day?"

He says, "You don't know Independent Day?"

I'm thinking, These guys come in for haircuts, it's gonna be good. I'll go.

He says, "Let's meet up by the shop and then we'll ride to Hollywood. That's about nine or ten miles. We'll go in a big group to the park. We'll have a barbecue."

On the day of the ride, as soon as we pull out of the shop, I see they're carrying big bags. I say, "What's that for?"

Avi says, "That's for the event."

I say, "Should I have brought something?"

He says, "Oh, no. We've got everything here. Don't worry about it."

They pull up, about seven or eight motorcycles, *Vrrrummm*. Then we stop at this Starbucks and there's like thirty or forty people there. As soon as we pull up there, I realize everyone is from Israel. And then I realize this is a parade about Israel.

So this guy comes out with a megaphone and he says, "Hey, people. Who's new here?"

I say, "Me."

He says, "You! Come up front."

I say, "What's going on?"

He says, "You want to ride up front?"

So they take my motorcycle, and they take these Israeli flags, and they decorate it completely. I'm thinking, Oh, my God, what's going on here?"

He says, "All right, you're going to be up front. I'll ride your bike and you're going to be standing on the back with the flags."

I say, "Flags?"

He says, "Yeah! It's the Independence Day of Israel. That's what the ride is for, right?"

I'm like, "What?"

I say, "Avi, what the fuck? Why didn't you tell me? I'm Muslim!"

Avi says, "That's all right, don't worry about it."

I say, "What do you mean, don't worry about it!"

He says, "Don't say anything to anybody. They might get upset."

I say, "*They* might get upset?"

My bike is decorated with Israeli flags, there's no way I can back out now.

So the leader gives me two

Israeli flags and says, "You hold them up."

I'm thinking, Well, I guess I'm gonna do it. What the hell? Let's do it.

This pickup truck pulls right in front of us. I say, "What's that pickup for?"

He says, "Oh, all the TV channels and newspaper photographers are going to ride in that."

I say, "You've got to be kidding me."

He says, "You're gonna be on TV. It's gonna be good. You're gonna be in front!"

I can't back out. Here I am. I have these flags. I have a hundred Israelis behind me and I'm on a TV station. Everybody's cheering, weeping.

We get to this park. The park has got a couple thousand people. I'm so nervous someone's going to start a conversation with me and say, "He's not Israeli." I'm trying not to talk to anyone. I'm thinking, as soon as we get to the park, I'll take off with my bike. Nobody will care. People are going to start drinking soon anyway.

I get there. The president's a big guy. He holds me by the neck and says, "You did great, kid. You were awesome." He's American and he's never been to Israel. But he's very passionate about Israel. So I'm like okay, good, he's not going to pick up on me.

He says, "Avi tells me you cut all these guys' hair."

I say, "Yes, I do."

He says, "I should come to you for a haircut."

I say, "Sure."

So he comes for a haircut and he's sitting at my station and he says, "I love my haircut. I should have met you years ago. My son's *upsherin* is coming up." Jewish people have a ceremony, when a kid turns three. It's the first haircut. Glen says, "I want you to come for the ceremony. For my kid."

But he never told me I would cut the hair.

He says, "I would be really personally so upset if you don't show up, after everything you have done for the parade and the community."

I come home and tell my friend, "We need to buy a yamaka."

She says, "Why do you need a yamaka? You're a Muslim."

I say, "Don't even ask. I got myself into something I can't bail out of."

I ask a couple of Jewish friends, they're laughing. I get the yamaka and here I go to the synagogue. At the synagogue, they are very welcoming. They say, "Oscar, thank you so much for coming. Did you bring your scissors?"

I say, "Why would I need my scissors?"

Glen says, "You're gonna cut the hair. What's the matter with you? Don't you know?"

I say, "Hair?"

Glen says, "Don't worry about it. We'll find a scissors." So they find like a regular scissors. Here comes the ceremony, and they're chanting and singing. It's very solemn. I come in with the yamaka, I cut the hair, and everyone is praying.

I'm thinking, Oh, my God, Oscar, sometimes you need to learn to say no.

Investing in Sexy Pictures

I received an e-mail for an appointment and I think, Who fuckin' emails to make an appointment? But this guy did.

I don't remember his exact name. Let's call him Andrew. Andrew calls me and says he's moving to Florida from the West Coast and he's just getting divorced.

I'm like, Okay.

He's been going to the same barber for 25 years and Andrew says it's hard for him to find a barber. Somehow he got my information through the internet and he wants to give me a shot.

I say, "I work with appointments. You're welcome to come in any time, as long as I know you're coming."

He says, "Great!"

So we set up an appointment and in he comes. He actually was in his late 40s, but was much younger looking. One of those California guys. He's got short hair, fairly simple, blondish. There was something unique about him. He's got that cool, techie-guy vibe, you know?

He sits in my chair, I cut his hair, and we hit it off right away. He liked the haircut and he kept coming back, time after time.

He always talked about his work. I guess he wanted to forget about his personal problems. One day, he comes in and says, "Hey, Oscar, a bunch of guys I work with have developed something we think is going to be a major social media company."

I say, "Okay, how does it work?"

He says, "You send a picture to someone and you can make that picture last in their phone as long as you want."

I'm like, "What does that mean?"

He says, "I send you a picture and you can only look at it for as long as I want you to. It can be 3 seconds, 5 seconds, 10 seconds, one minute, one day. I get to pick how long you can look at that picture. How long can you see it."

I was like, "So if a girl wants to send a sexy picture to a guy or if kids want to exchange inappropriate pictures that they don't want to hang around, it's something like that."

Andrew says, "Basically, yeah.

We've developed this thing so the girls can send the pictures and they will only last 3 seconds. The girls are sure of it. It will be something like that. We're looking for investors. You can join us for as little as a thousand bucks for 5% of the company. These guys are really strapped for money."

I say, "Dude, first, I don't believe that people should send each other naked pictures or inappropriate pictures, or whatever reason they're going to use this idea. Secondly, I'm not a big investor guy. Actually, I don't have any money. It's not something for me."

Andrew says, "Are you sure about this? I think these guys are really onto something."

I say, "It's not my thing, man."

Two, three months go by, and Andrew says, "Hey, Oscar! I hate to tell you, but I'm going to move back to California."

I say, "Why is that?"

He says, "I met this beautiful girl. I've been dating her. I've got a kid, and she's got a kid. She wants to move to California. She got a really good job offer and I'm gonna have to go with her and follow my heart once again."

I'm like, "Dude, it was a pleasure meeting you. Life is yours. I was so happy to meet you. You're a very interesting guy."

We kept in touch after he left. Today, Andrew is running the websites for a major cell phone provider. He must be in his early 50s.

He sends me an email maybe a year after he moved to California. It says something like, "Oscar, do you know how big the offer was that Facebook made for that social media company? THREE BILLION! And that company turned it down, because the CEO says it's worth even more!"

I email back, "I know. I don't want to talk about it."

Those guys Andrew knew, that he wanted me to invest with, their company is now worth ten billion dollars. I could have turned that $1,000 investment into millions of dollars, but I didn't.

I say to myself, I guess it wasn't meant to be.

Judging a Book by Its Cover

We had this barbershop and we'd just opened. It was a hot summer day and Don comes in. He's sweating, he has long hair. He didn't look like a professional journalist, as least not my idea of one.

He says, "I work for the Sun Sentinel and here's my business card" and I think, Dude, you don't even comb your hair.

He says, "I've heard about you. If you have a moment, I'd like to interview you and do a write-up on you."

People in the shop are looking at him and saying to one another, "This guy is not a journalist."

I say, "In a couple of days, call me back and we'll set up an appointment."

Everybody heard me in this shop and they say, "Dude, you just wasted ten minutes. He's not going to write about you. He's wasting your time."

I say, "Look, if he comes, it's great. He'll do a write-up. If he doesn't come, what's the big deal? Don't judge a book by its cover. I do this for a living. I know people."

Sure enough, Don shows up. He's got a notebook. He's asking me about barbering. I had these model cars, he's asking about those. He gathered as much information as he could.

He says, "I'm going to do the write-up and when it's published, I'll bring you a copy."

I'm thinking, Great. I can put it in my window. I can frame it.

Everybody in the shop again says, "Oscar, that guy's not a journalist. That's all bullshit. He just wanted to talk to you."

I'm like, "What do you guys know? Are you experts on journalists? You have radar that tells you who's a journalist and who isn't? The guy asked me a bunch of questions. Why would he ask them if he wasn't a real journalist?"

They say, "He's just wasting your time."

I say, "He's the real thing. I know people."

Maybe a month later, Don calls me. He says, "Hey, your story is going to be in the newspaper. On Thursday. Page two. Make sure you read it."

I'm like, I was right! He's really going to do a story on me. I tell everyone in the shop, "See! I told you!"

They say, "Let's wait for Thursday."

Thursday, I'm right there on the page. Don took a picture of me. I cut that story out and I put it on my window.

As soon as I put it on my window, I saw people stopping and reading it. They'd open the door and ask, "Who's Oscar?"

I'm like, "That's me."

They'd ask, "Can I get a haircut with Oscar the Barber?"

Everybody started calling me Oscar the Barber. It's amazing how people look at publishing.

I'd watch the people from inside the shop, and I'd tell everyone in the shop, "Look, that man is going to read Don's article and then he's going to come in here for a haircut." It happened every time: These guys would be walking, stopping, reading, thinking, Oh, wow, he's in the newspaper, he must be good. And they'd come in for a haircut.

That article boosted my business big time and I was Oscar the Barber after that.

And then Don began coming to me as a client. I think he's very impressed that I use a straight razor. I'm one of the few barbers who still uses one. I take pride in it. I finish with a neck shave. That's old school.

If you make a haircut just a haircut, it's so what? There are so many barbers. What makes me different? I studied psychology for two years. What makes something memorable is the emotion attached to it. If I turn a haircut into an experience, if I really care about my clients, they'll feel loyal. I check on my customers. I call them. If they tell me they will have medical tests, I'll put a note in my book to find out how they are.

When a guy like Don comes into my chair, I want to meet his expectations. We have a good relationship. His article brought me many customers.

And I got all that because I refused to judge a book by its cover.

The Cool Father and Son

Josh, this father, has been coming to me for a long time. He starts coming to me weekly. He says, "I want to bring my son in here, but he doesn't want to come to you."

I say, "Why?"

He says, "He thinks you're just an old guy. If he came one time, he'd know and he'd like you."

I say, "Tell him to come."

The father says, "How about if I pre-pay for his haircut and then tell him you're going to give him a complimentary haircut on Saturday?"

"Done! Deal! Set it up."

So on Saturday, I see his son David come in and I realize he's been coming to me for three years.

I say, "David! What are you doing here? You don't have an appointment."

He says, "Yes, I do. My dad paid for it. My dad kept saying I should come to his barber, that he was a cool guy and I'm thinking, Oh, Dad, come on. He must be some old fart."

Finally, they realized they'd *both* been coming to me for a long time.

Many years later, David, the son,

is an attorney. The father still comes to me. Now they both come for haircuts early in the morning.

The father calls one day and he says, "Can you cut my hair at 8:30?"

I say, "Not this Saturday, I can't do it at 8:30. I have other regular customers. How about if you come at 8:15? Your son can come a little later."

Josh was very upset. I couldn't understand why he was so upset. So I call his son, David, and David says, "Dude, I don't want to get up that early to get a haircut at eight in the morning. I want to sleep in."

I say, "David, it's not the haircut. I think your father wants to spend the time with you in the shop. Because that's the only time you really have together."

He says, "Yeah, man, that just hit me, too."

So I called them up and say, "I'll open the shop a little early. Why don't you guys come at 8 o'clock?"

Josh was so happy. He was in the parking lot at quarter to 8, waiting for me. His son comes, and Josh's eyes pop and he says, "Oh, my God. My son!" If you could have seen the light in his eyes.

That moment – cutting a father and son's hair – that's the amazing part of my job. That's when I love my job.

The Funky Lady

I have this lady client who comes to me. Jennifer's a funky lady, in her mid-forties. I do cut some ladies' hair, but not a lot. The women have to be a customer's wife or sister or some other family member. I want to stick to barbering. I cut Jennifer's husband's hair.

One day I say to Jennifer, "How did you guys meet each other?"

She says, "We met in high school. I knew all along that we belonged to each other and that we will love each other for the rest of our lives. When we finished high school, I looked at Johnson and I said, 'You know, I've got a feeling that we're going to be together and we'll spend our retirement years together. However, I want to go out and experience life on my own first and you should do the same thing. Even though I love you and you love me, we should break up.'

"He's like, 'What do you mean, break up? We're going to college.'"

Jennifer says, "I'm telling you, it's not going to work like this."

So they break up. He goes on,

gets married. She goes on, gets married. Ten, twelve years later, she gets up in the morning and she says to herself, "It's time to call Johnson."

I say, "How did that idea come to you?"

Jennifer says, "I don't know. I woke up one morning, and something inside of me said, 'It's time to call Johnson.'"

I say, "That's very interesting. What did you do?"

She says, "I opened the Yellow Pages, I found his phone number. I called him up."

I say, "Did he answer?"

She says, "Yep. I said to him, 'Hey, this is Jennifer.' Johnson is like, 'What do you mean, Jennifer? Which Jennifer?'"

She says, "How many Jennifers do you know, God damn it? There's only supposed to be one."

He says, "Man, it's been how many years? Ten years, twelve years I haven't heard from you? I'm married."

She says, "So am I. This is what we're gonna do. We're gonna move to Florida, you're gonna divorce your wife and I'm gonna divorce my husband. I'm gonna find a job and I'm gonna move us there."

Within one year, they'd divorced their spouses and they'd moved to Florida and they got married here. They're both my clients now. It's amazing that she knew all along they would be together.

I say to Johnson, "How did you know that you were going to leave your wife because someone calls you ten years later?"

He says, "Dude, she made me promise."

I say, "That's a heavy promise to hold."

The Merry Christmas

A Jewish customer comes in on Christmas Eve. I'm closing the shop. He says, "I need to get a haircut."

I'm like, "Look, dude, I'm closing. It's Christmas Eve. I have stuff to do."

He says, "Come on. One more haircut."

I'm thinking, Okay, it's Christmas Eve. I'll do something good.

I say, "Come on in, sit down." I cut his hair, he's a great guy from Canada. A successful businessman. We hit it off well. This guy's pretty cool.

As he gets ready to pay he says, "I love that gel you put on me. What is it?"

I say, "I sell it here. It's my number one seller."

He says, "Can I get one of those gels?"

I say, "Sure," and I give him one.

I ring him up and he says, "Shoot! I don't have any money on me. I live down the street. Let me walk home and come back."

I say, "It's Christmas Eve. I can't wait another half hour here."

He says, "I'm leaving for
Canada. How am I gonna pay you?"

I say, "It's Christmas Eve. Merry
Christmas!"

He says, "But I'm Jewish."

I say, "So what? I'm Muslim.
Keep the hair gel. Forget about the
haircut. Have a great day. Christmas
is still merry."

I used to smoke and I'm
standing outside the shop one day
and this Ferrari pulls up. I love cars,
and this is like the newest hot, red
Ferrari. This guy gets out and he says,
"Oscar, right? Do you remember me?"

I say, "No, but I want to know
everything about you *and* the car!"

He says, "I'm the Jewish guy
who came on a Christmas Eve and
didn't have any money and you gave
me gel and a haircut. Well, Merry
Christmas to you. Take her for a spin."

He gives me the keys for the
Ferrari. I say, "Really?"

He says, "Things in life happen
unexpectedly. Now you know how I
feel."

So we took a spin and he's been
a great customer since then.

The Billionaire

This customer is a short, stocky guy. He's very interesting, very quirky and very quiet.

When you look at him, you know he is somebody. He's been coming to me for a long time. He's a very successful older guy. I realized how successful after I saw him in *Forbes* magazine. He was one of the top fifty richest people.

I texted him and said, "George, I didn't realize you were one of the top 50 in *Forbes*."

He says, "Where?"

I say, "*Forbes* magazine. They've got your picture."

He says, "Yeah, I do pretty good." He was so humble.

He always says to me, "Oscar, I admire your ambition."

I'm thinking, here's this guy who's a billionaire. He sits in my chair. I cut his hair. And he's so taken with me. He keeps saying, "Oscar, you're amazingly enthusiastic." He likes my ambition and enthusiasm.

He happens to be close friends with the President of the United States. He says, "If I get a chance, I'll get you in the door, and you'll get to meet him."

I say, "How are we gonna meet him?"

He says, "He usually sits in the pool on Sundays and eats ice cream. I can get you in for a two-minute conversation while he's eating his ice cream. That will make your day."

I hope it happens some day.

His humbleness is amazing. He'll want to make an appointment and I'll say I can't do it at that time and he'll say, "That's okay. What you do is very special. You tell me what time to come."

People like him, very successful people, they don't worry about money. They focus on relationships and the mission. That's one thing I learned from them. Focusing on money takes you away from your mission.

He always tells me, "Do what you do best. The money will just come. Stay ambitious. I envy you your ambition."

The Woman with the Shaved Head

I have this customer who comes in all the time and one day his wife calls. She says, "Oscar, can I make an appointment with you? Do you do head shaves?"

I say, "Head shaves? Yeah."

She says, "Could you shave my head?"

I say, "Your head?"

She says, "Yeah, I've got cancer. I wear these wigs and they are hot, so I like to keep my head shaved."

I say, "Come on in."

Her name was Rose, and she was such a beautiful woman. She was in her late sixties, but she looked like she was thirty-five. The way she carried herself, she was like a super model.

When she came into the shop, I'd make her feel as comfortable as possible.

The first time she came in, I say, "We're gonna shave you with a straight razor, okay?"

She says, "What do you mean?"

I say, "It will give you the smoothest shave." So I shaved her and she felt her head and said, "Oh, wow, that's very smooth."

She liked it. She started coming once a week to get her head shaved and her husband is still coming to me once a month. One day she says, "I'm really having a problem with a port on my arm. Something's wrong, like an infection or something. I have to go to Miami, to the hospital. I don't think I can make my next haircut."

I say, "That's okay, Rose. We'll shave your head when you come back."

Then she calls me at the last minute and says, "Oscar, can you shave my head before I go?"

She comes in – she loved her husband very much and he loved her. They had this very deep connection. She was so worried during that visit that if she died, her husband wouldn't move on. She was tired. She kept saying, "I just can't keep doing this any more. I know it's going to come to an end soon."

I kept saying, "No, don't talk that way. Keep fighting. Keep your spirits up."

So off she goes to Miami, to the hospital. I texted her and told her to

be strong. Rose texted me, "Take care
of my husband as much as you can.
Tell him good things about me."

Then I don't hear from her. Later
that week, I get this text message from
her husband. He says, "We lost Rose."

The husband calls me and says,
"Hey, we're doing a get-together for
Rose. Do you want to come for a
cocktail?"

I say, "Of course. I was so taken
by her."

The couple was very social. They
know a lot of famous, powerful
people. Her husband said he was
keeping the gathering very small, "Just
for the special people." I promised to
be there.

I went there. She had three
beautiful kids. Each one looks like a
super model. Rose's husband says,
"Oscar, I want you to come and see
something."

Before Rose passed away, she
did a collage. She put in moments
with the people most special to her.
My picture was there, too. We took
that picture during a head shave and
sent it to the kids. Knowing all those
people for sixty years or more, she
gave me a little piece in the collage. It

touched my heart.

The Good Husband

Joe has been coming to me for a long time. Joe and his wife, Renee, would both come into the shop. She used to get her hair cut by one of the stylists. I used to cut his hair. Renee was a beautiful lady and Joe was a good-looking man. They were super happy. You could tell they were madly in love. They lifted everyone's spirits when they came into the shop.

One day, I say, "Hi, Renee. Come have a seat here."

She looks at me like she didn't understand what I was saying. I couldn't figure her out. I say, "Oh, my God. Are you okay?"

She says, "I don't know. What am I supposed to do?"

I say, "What do you mean? Sit."

She says, "I don't know. I don't know." She seemed lost. And she was a young woman.

I took her arm and helped her sit in the chair.

Her husband comes in and I tell him what happened and ask, "Is your wife okay?"

He says, "Yeah, man, she forgets stuff lately and I'm concerned. We went to a doctor and unfortunately she's got Alzheimer's."

I say, "She's only fifty years old."

Her husband says, "I know. The doctor says sometimes it starts early. There's nothing we can do, Oscar. Absolutely nothing. You know what sucks? We love each other so much. We were high school sweethearts. We went together in college."

Something happened – I don't know why they broke up. But they went different ways in life. Joe says, "Years later, I move into this condo and I come out and there she is, next to me. I say, 'Oh, my God, Renee, what are you doing here?' She's like, 'My husband and I, we got divorced. I got this condo.'"

Joe says to her, "My wife and I, we just got divorced and I just got *this* condo."

They couldn't believe it. They were next-door neighbors. Joe says to her, "Didn't you know I was moving in?" She had no idea. The universe brought them back together.

So they decided, "Let's give it another shot." They're madly in love, they get married, and then they get hit by this Alzheimer's thing.

Joe and Renee continued to be our clients until her last days. He used to come every two or three weeks, whenever Renee needed her nails done or her hair done. He used to bring her into the shop. It was amazing. As the disease went on, Renee didn't know how to sit, she didn't know what to do, she couldn't talk. But you'd look at her and she was beautiful.

It used to hit her sometimes – that something was wrong. I'd see her crying while she got her hair cut. She knew she was sick. She was so embarrassed that she had Alzheimer's.

Joe never gave up on her. Ever.

She passed away. He still comes to me for haircuts.

I ask him, "Hey, man, how do you feel?"

He says, "Oscar, I love her. I still love her so much."

They were married about five years when she got sick. Joe can't believe the universe brought them together and she gets Alzheimer's disease. He dealt with it for fifteen years. He cleaned her, he took care of her, he put his entire life on hold.

Their love must have been so

passionate. He says, "Oscar, those five years I lived with her were worth ten lifetimes."

The Shelby Mustang

I have this customer, Dwayne, who came from money. His family had a successful business and he worked in it. He actually survived an airplane crash. He was so lucky, he was the only person to survive the crash. He lives in the Midwest. He doesn't want to fly, so he drives for two days for a haircut.

He says, "Oscar, you are the only guy who cuts my hair. I love the way you cut my hair. To me, it's worth it to drive two days to get a haircut."

So one day, he's very upset. I say, "Dwayne, what's wrong?"

He says, "I've got cancer. In my spine."

I say, "Wow, that's not good."

He goes through the surgery and the doctors tell him he has a year to live. He finds this therapy and he's still alive after six years. Whatever he's doing, it's keeping him alive.

So he comes to me and he's a little down. "Man, I'm trying to do everything I can and I'm not having fun."

I say, "Dwayne, what the heck is wrong with you? You've got all the money in the world. You're a lucky son of a bitch. You survived a plane crash. Doctors told you you're supposed to be dead in a year – it's been six-seven years and you don't show any signs of any illness. Enjoy your life. Do something you've always wanted to do!"

He says, "You know what, man? You are so right!"

I pumped him up, man. He got out of that barber shop a happy man.

He calls me four hours later and says, "Hey, Oscar, this is Dwayne."

I say, "What's up?"

He says, "Hey, man, I'm at the Ford dealership. I just bought a Ford Shelby Mustang."

I say, "Okay."

The problem is he walks into the dealership, and says he wants a Shelby Mustang today. The salesman says, "What do you mean?"

Dwayne says, "What part don't you understand? I want to buy a Shelby Mustang. Today."

The salesman says, "Okay, what color do you want?"

Dwayne says, "I don't care. I just want a Shelby."

The salesman says, "We have

one. A purple one."

Dwayne says, "I'll take it. Write it up."

So the salesman writes it up, he brings the car around and Dwayne gets into the car. The car is a stick shift.

Dwayne says, "Dude, I don't know how to drive a stick."

The salesman says, "Shelbys only come in stick."

Dwayne says, "What am I going to do?"

The salesman says, "I can drive it to your home."

Dwayne says, "Maybe we can drive to Oscar's barber shop, so he can drive me home."

So he calls me at the barber shop and says, "Dude, I just bought a Shelby."

I say, "Why would you do that?"

He says, "You told me, 'Go out there. You got the money. Do something you've always wanted to do.'"

So he comes to the shop and says, "After I signed the papers, I realized I don't know how to drive this car. The guy says I have to take it home. It's my car. Oscar, I don't know how to drive it home.

"The only reason I got this car is I wanna put the top down and I wanna go a hundred and twenty, a hundred and fifty miles an hour and I wanna feel that breeze."

He looked at me like he wanted it now. Like that's why he got that impulse to buy the car. He was planning on getting out of the dealership and riding it hard.

I say, "I'll tell you what. I'll drive."

Dwayne says, "Really? I want to see what this car can do."

I say, "Sure. Hop in."

He's got a Dunkin' Donuts coffee in his hand and I say, "Dwayne, you may want to put that on the side of the door."

He says, "Why?"

"Because we're gonna go fast. You don't want it on you."

He says, "You're sure?"

The Shelby was a fast car. I couldn't shift fast enough to catch up with the speed. Here we are on A1A, going seventy, eighty miles an hour, with the exhaust roaring. The whole neighborhood knows it's a new car. We come to a red light, I look at his face. He's so happy, like a fat kid in a chocolate shop.

He got such a high on that drive, he's shaking like a leaf. I say, "Dwayne, you okay?"

He says, "I should have done this years ago!"

He takes a drink and he's shaking so much from the adrenaline he pours coffee all over himself. I say, "Dwayne, relax."

We had to stop and buy him a T-shirt because he had coffee all over his shirt. He says, "You got to drive this to my condo."

Then he learns how to drive the Shelby.

Next haircut he comes in with his car and I say, "How come the top is up?"

He says, "The second top doesn't fit so well."

I say, "Second? What happened to the first top?"

He says, "I was driving through the Everglades. I wanted that adrenaline again. I put the top down and I smashed the gas pedal. Smashed it! And all of a sudden *POP!* This big noise. The top just came off the car. Just came off. The whole thing."

The Revenge of the Rich Girl

Joshua had been coming to me for a long time. He was single. He used to date a lot of girls and we used to talk about it. After one date he says, "There's this hot chick from Miami."

I'm like, "Yeah?"

He says, "She is smokin' hot. And she's rich. And she's totally into me."

I'm like, "Cool."

He managed this building and he says, "She lives in the building. We have a company policy. I cannot associate with residents."

I'm like, "That sucks."

He says, "We are so afraid it's going to come out and I'm going to lose my job."

I say, "Don't do anything crazy. Take it easy."

Next haircut, he says, "Dude, that girl. I told you she was so rich. She sold her condo in the building I manage and she bought another unit in another building so we can be together."

I say, "Wow! That is amazing."

He says, "Oscar, this girl, I want you to meet her. This is it."

I say, "Great."

Now this guy he comes for a haircut, I see him like fifteen minutes a month. He says, "Can we go out? Can we go out?"

I say, "Sure."

We went out – two couples – had dinner, one hour, an hour and fifteen minutes, maybe. She was a cool chick. We had a great time. Everybody went home.

Next week, Joshua comes in and says to me, "Dude, I can't keep up with this girl."

"Why? What happened?"

"Oh, my God, Oscar," he says. "When we go out, we go to fancy restaurants with her friends. I can't afford them. Her friends will say, 'Let's all have champagne. You okay with that, Joshua?'

"I'm like, 'Sure.' They order a seven-hundred-dollar-bottle of champagne. I can't afford that! I make fifty grand a year." He kept complaining about it – he couldn't keep up, he couldn't keep up.

So I say, "Dude, if you are not happy. If you feel beneath her. If things aren't working out, take the high road and say, 'I'm going to get someone on my level.' Or just forget about the money. Because it doesn't seem to bother her. She seems okay with it. She comes from a rich family. Don't worry about it."

Next month he comes back again and says, "I don't think I can keep going out with her. What do you think? What do you think? You know people. You've met her."

I say, "Dude, you seem to be so worried about it. If you don't want to be with her, stop talking to her. Don't talk to her on the phone. Don't answer her text messages. You guys don't live together."

He says, "You think I should do that?"

I say, "I don't know, but if you don't want to be with her, don't go out with her."

"Okay," he says.

Next morning, I get a text message from the girlfriend. She says, "Oscar, I can't believe you made Joshua and my relationship come to an end. How dare you break us up!"

I texted back, "Break you up? I don't know anything about this. I just cut Joshua's hair. Leave me alone."

I get a phone call from an

attorney's office. The attorney left a voice mail message. It said, "This message is for Mr. Oscar Alci. I'm calling from the US Customs and Immigration Enforcement." That's ICE! The lawyer says, "Someone has complained about your immigration status. You'd better get yourself a lawyer."

I'm thinking, What a dumb girl. She doesn't realize I'm an American citizen. Because I have an accent she thought I was some immigrant working without a green card.

I called her a couple of times. She didn't call me back. Unfortunately, Joshua stopped coming to me for a haircut. He took my advice and broke up with the girlfriend and put the blame on me.

The Man with One Eyebrow

It's midday, I'm in the shop, and I'm working with a couple of people. This guy, Steve, comes in and asks, "How much is a haircut?"

I say, "Sixteen dollars." That's what it cost back then.

He says, "Oof, $16, that's above my budget."

I say, "No problem, there are other places."

He says, "Do I have to tip you on top of it?"

I say, "Normally, people leave a couple of extra dollars for a tip."

He says, "How about if I pay you $14 for a haircut? And I'll give you a $2 tip? That's a total of $16."

I say, "But the haircut is $16. You can just pay me $16 for the haircut and don't tip me."

"Oh, no," he says, "I'd feel bad not tipping you."

I say, "Well, a haircut is $16. If you give me $16 I'm going to accept that as $16, not as you gave me $14 and a $2 tip."

He says, "I just want a haircut."

I say, "I know you just want a haircut. I'm just telling you how I'm

going to accept that $16." So we go
back and forth and I say, "Why don't
you sit down and I'll cut your hair."

So I start cutting his hair and he
says, "Are you going to do my
eyebrows, too?"

And I say, "Sure, I'll trim your
eyebrows."

He says, "Knowing you, you
probably charge extra for the
eyebrows."

I don't charge anything for the
eyebrows, but I think, This guy is
nickel-and-diming me for everything I
do. I was going to tell him to forget it,
but he was so insistent, so sarcastic,
that I kept it going.

I say, "I will charge you a dollar
per eyebrow."

He says, "You gotta be kidding
me."

I say, "Why would I kid you if I
am seriously answering a question?
One dollar an eyebrow."

He says, "I don't know. I don't
know. They look really bushy, but I
don't know."

As he's talking I'm saying, "Do
you want me to cut them? Do you
want me to cut them?" I'm really
putting on the pressure. "Make up

your mind. I've got people waiting."

He says, "Go ahead and cut it."

I cut one eyebrow and I'm going to do the other eyebrow and he says, "Hold on, hold on. I have to give you 17 bucks now, because of that eyebrow."

I say, "Yes."

He says, "Don't trim the other one."

I say, "What do you mean?"

He says, "Don't touch my other eyebrow."

I'm like, "Are you serious?"

He says, "I don't want to pay an extra dollar for one eyebrow. When I go home, I'll trim my own eyebrow."

So I say, "For ONE DOLLAR, you're gonna leave this shop with one eyebrow trimmed and the other very bushy looking?"

He says, "Yeah! Absolutely."

He paid me $17, no tip, and left with one eyebrow trimmed.

The Harley-Davidson

This couple has been coming to me for a long time. His name was Prescott and his partner's name was Christopher. Prescott was a big, heavyset guy, well-spoken. Chris was well-spoken, thin and athletic, maybe 20 years younger than Prescott.

These two guys, they were the coolest guys. Prescott made Chris give me a call. I remember it like it was yesterday.

Chris says, "Hi, is this Oscar? I want to bring my friend, Prescott, for a haircut. Can you make an appointment?"

I say, "Sure."

He says, "Are you usually on time with your appointments?"

I say, "I take pride in being on time."

He says, "Oh, my God. Prescott is going to love you."

When I have a new customer, I allow an extra two-three minutes. I like to see what they're driving, how they're coming in. I want to go out and welcome them into my shop so they feel very welcome.

Prescott had a big 7 series BMW,

decked out. He's sitting in the back and Chris was driving the car. I told Chris, I thought he was a helper, a driver. I didn't know they were a couple at first.

Prescott was a big dude and he's got these black sunglasses on and this beautiful aftershave. I believe it was Hermes. He had a hard time walking, so he would touch Chris's shoulder and kind of like walk behind him.

Prescott sits in my chair and he says, "Well, sweetheart, tell me about yourself."

I say, "I'm from Istanbul, Turkey. I've been doing hair for a long time. I'm glad you came in here."

He says, "Yes, that's great. Sweetheart, I feel like you're an artist. Make me look beautiful."

And I'm looking at this guy, and he's like older and heavyset but he's so genuine.

He says, "Do what you think is right for me."

So I give him a basic cut and he liked it. He says, "Sweetheart, I love your haircut. Chris! Pay the man."

So Chris pays me the money, with a good, hefty tip, and they leave.

Time after time they came in and

I got to know them a little. I found out that Prescott was a very, very famous art dealer. Dealing art that cost millions of dollars. He deliberately bought a condo with heavy security. Inside, there was more security.

In time, as we became friends, he realized that I like motorcycles. One day he came into the shop and he says, "Sweetheart, you like motorcycles, don't you?"

I say, "Yes, I do."

He says, "If you were to say, 'One motorcycle is my dream,' what would that be?"

I say, "What's the difference, if dreams are not going to come true?"

He says, "You never know, sweetheart. What would be the best motorcycle you can think of?"

I say, "I guess it would be a Harley-Davidson."

He says, "Oscar, sweetheart, you deserve a Harley-Davidson."

I say, "Thank you."

He says, "Chris, come here. You're gonna buy Oscar a motorcycle and you're gonna get it painted special."

I say, "I don't want a motorcycle from you."

He says, "Why not?

I say, "Why would you want to buy me a motorcycle?"

He says, "You're a great guy and you do a great job on my hair and I have enough and I want to share it with you."

I say, "No, I can't accept such a big gift."

He says, "Sweetheart, you're a very nice guy" and he leaves the shop.

Next time he comes in he says, "Sweetheart, I got something for you."

I say, "Don't tell me you bought me a motorcycle."

He says, "You tell me what you think of it. Chris, call the guys. You got a minute, sweetheart?"

So we go outside and there's a flatbed with a brand-new Harley-Davidson on it. I'm looking at this motorcycle and thinking, Oh, my gosh, is that mine?

I say, "Why the hell did you buy a motorcycle and plant it in front of my place?"

He says, "I want your artistic opinion."

I say, "About what?"

He says, "What do you think would work on this motorcycle?"

I say, "I don't know. You could put flames on it, maybe some skulls to make it dramatic." So I gave him a couple of ideas about it.

He says to me, "Okay, sweetheart."

I found out, a couple of months later, that he's very sick. His partner calls me and says, "Oscar, Prescott is very, very sick and he wants to see you. Would you come to our condo to cut his hair one last time?"

I say, "Wow, I wondered what had happened to you guys. I hadn't heard from you for a long time."

So I go to their place, I go through like five different security people. I come to this door. I'm expecting like, Wow! I'm wondering, What does this guy's condo look like?

It's on the 30th floor in a skyscraper on the beach. I go in there, ring the bell and *ding!* this door opens and I see two huge, super-masculine football-player-type dudes. I'm like, Oh, my God, what's going on in here?

I soon realize that they were Prescott's help. Two huge body builder guys. Their arms were like so huge.

Inside was a huge painting, like

50 by 50. It covered the entire wall. Prescott says, "Sweetheart, is that you?"

I'm like, "Yes, it's me."

He says, "Come on over here."

I go to his room. He's sleeping in a hospital bed. He says, "Oscar, thank you very much for coming and taking care of me. I really, really appreciate it."

I say, "Prescott, I don't usually go to people's houses and cut their hair. Therefore, I consider you a friend and I'm not going to charge you for it."

He says, "No, no, I have to give you some money."

I say, "No, that's not how my principles work. I'm not going to charge you any money."

He says, "Fine. How are you going to cut my hair?"

I say, "Well, we're going to have to sit you in a chair."

He says, "No, sweetheart, I'll get that taken care of."

He calls these big goons. They sit him up and they're holding him, one on each side. And he's a big guy. I told them, "Guys, this haircut is going to take like 15 minutes."

They say, "We don't care."

Prescott says, "Sweetheart, that's what I pay them for. Let them get tired."

I worked as quick as possible and I made him as presentable as possible. Then I said, "Well, I wish you all the luck." I didn't know what else to say.

He says, "Sweetheart, I still have that motorcycle painted the way you like it, in my garage. If you want it, one more chance, it's yours."

I say, "Prescott, I really, really cannot accept it. But I really appreciate it."

He says, "Oscar, you're a true artist. Just keep doing what you do and don't let anyone get in front of you."

He passed away maybe a month later.

Why didn't I accept the motorcycle?

How can I accept a $30,000 motorcycle? I grew up poor. What's he going to ask me in return?

I have customers who give me huge tips. One guy says, "Oscar, the amount of money I'm giving you is nothing to me. But you can take your wife out for a beautiful dinner. Take it."

Okay, I'll take it. But I always tell them, "Don't call me and expect the royal treatment. I'm going to treat you the same as a guy who doesn't tip me at all."

The Woman Who Would Not Dye

This lady walks into the shop. I'd say she's in her sixties. She's got fairly short hair. As soon as she comes in, she says, "Can I get a haircut and can I get hair color?"

"Yeah, sure," I say.

She says, "I'm not going to ask you how much it is, because I have never paid for a haircut and color in my life."

I say, "Why? You used to do hair? You owned a hair salon?"

She says, "No, every hair salon I go to, I make a deal with the stylist. You see my white hair? I want my hair black. But somehow no hair dresser and no barber can color my hair. My hair never takes the color. I always make a deal – if you can't do a good color job, I'm not going to pay for the haircut. No one can dye my hair."

I'm looking at this woman and she's got white hair. I do this kind of coloring all day long. I tell myself, Oscar, you know how to do this. I talk to the people in the salon. They say, "Oh, Oscar, just put the frickin' color on."

I tell the lady, "Sit down. I'm gonna do your color."

She says, "Good."

So I mix the color as dark as possible. As dark as it can get. I put it on the hair. I actually use extra drops, they call them GOD drops – that's Gray Oxidizing Drops – for hair that is resistant to being colored. I figure no way this isn't going to work. I usually leave the color on 30 or 35 minutes. I left it on 50! I told her, "I've got this. I'm gonna be your new hairdresser. You're going to be coming to me for the rest of your life."

She says, "No, I don't think so."

I say, "Why are you so sure? I just put black dye on your hair."

She says, "I don't think it's gonna take."

Fifty minutes later I'm looking at her hair and her scalp is pitch black. I say, "It's time to wash."

She looks at me with a big grin and says, "You're gonna cut it for free, right? That's what you agreed."

I say, "No, it's colored. You're gonna pay for a haircut for the first time in your life."

She says, "I don't think so."

She's got this smile on her face.

We go to the shampoo bowl and I start washing her hair. As I wash it, she was right! All the color came out. Nothing stuck to the hair at all. I'm looking at her. I'm calling other people in the salon to come over to see this. No one can believe it.

I say to her, "Did you do something to your hair?"

She says, "Why would I do something? I've been trying to get my hair colored for years and years."

I'm thinking, there's something wrong with this. I'm wondering if she put something in her hair so she gets free haircuts and the color doesn't penetrate.

I say, "You know what? You got time? I'm going to try again."

She says, "I'm telling you, it's a waste of time."

I say, "No way!" I'd washed that hair. I'd blow-dried that hair. I took it personally.

I mix another round of color. Five-six people are around me now, all watching. Some are taking pictures. I say to them, "I washed the hair, that hair is clean. All I have to do is put the color on."

I take my time with the color.

She's laughing at me again, I'm praying, I add extra GOD drops. The time passes, I wash the hair. The color didn't stick to it at all. It was white again. I was shocked. So were the people around me. We couldn't believe the color was not taking.

She says to me, "How about my haircut?"

I cut her hair for free, I fix her up and I ask her, "What is this thing?"

She says, "I don't know. My hair turned gray, then white, in my late thirties."

A friend told her, "If you colored your hair, you would look younger." She started getting color at the grocery store and it didn't work. Nothing would color her hair. So somebody told her, "Maybe you're doing something wrong. Try going to a professional place to get your hair colored."

So she goes to one place, they can't color her hair. She goes to a second place, they can't color it. Third, fourth, fifth, sixth, seventh. No color. Her husband says to her, "If they can't do the job, they shouldn't charge you for it."

She says, "So I come up with the

idea of making a deal – a free haircut
if they can't color my hair." I gave her
a free haircut and she went to
challenge another salon.

The Tough Guy

Mack was from the Northeast. He was in charge of all the state prisons in a big state. He was retired and he would tell me what a tough job he had and how he'd had to deal with gang members, murderers. He spent his entire life dealing with the criminal world.

He had beautiful white hair and his wife had been cutting his hair for his entire life. But for some reason he wanted to spend time in South Florida and his wife had to go back home. His friends told him to come to me.

I told him the price of a haircut and he says, "Oh, my God. The last time I paid for a haircut it was like three or four dollars."

I say, "Where have you been living?"

He says, "Can I come with my grandson, Bobby, next time for a haircut?"

As tough as he looked and sounded, he wasn't a tough guy at all. His grandson had Down Syndrome. Bobby was in his thirties. Mack was in his seventies. He was 5-8, 5-9, his grandson was the same height, Mack was 160 pounds, his grandson was 180 pounds. Bobby couldn't walk. Mack used to put his grandson on his back and bring him into the shop.

When I first saw this, I say, "Mack, why not put your grandson in a wheelchair?"

Mack says, "He doesn't like wheelchairs." He never made his grandson feel that he was physically less than other people. He was so gentle with him.

The grandson could barely talk. He had his iPod on, and it was so loud I could hear it. The music was banging away.

I say to the grandkid, "Hey! You wanna haircut?"

He says, "Yes! Haircut! Oscar! Haircut!"

He was excited about the haircut and a super-nice guy. I'd shave his hair short and talk to him, "Hey, Bobby, how are you? How's everything going?"

The grandkid would say, "Oh, Bobby's happy. Happy! Hooooo!"

And something odd used to happen. Bobby would say, "Brrrrrrr! Phone! Phone!"

I'd say, "Why is he saying that,

Mack?"

Mack would say, "Your phone is gonna ring."

Ten seconds into it, my phone would ring.

I would say, "How does he know my phone is gonna ring?"

Mack says, "I don't know, Oscar. We sit home, we watch TV and all of a sudden he comes in the room and says, 'Brrrrr! Phone! Phone!' and the next thing you know, the phone is ringing."

I say, "Even if he's picking up the vibrations, he has on his headphones. They are so loud, I can hear the music!"

Mack says, "We never understand how he does it."

The last time Mack came for a haircut he looked sick. I think he had cancer and he didn't want to share it with his family. He says, "I'm very sick, Oscar. I want to spend my time with my Bobby."

I didn't hear from Mack and Bobby for like a year or two. I get a phone call from Mack's wife. I say, "How's Mack? I haven't heard from him. Is everything okay?"

She says, "Not necessarily. He

was crossing the street and he got hit
by a car and he died."

I say, "Oh, my God." My first
thought was the grandson. I say,
"Bobby must be devastated."

She says, "Bobby doesn't talk to
anybody any more. He doesn't listen
to his iPod any more. We want him to
get a haircut, but he gets very violent
and he doesn't want a haircut. I told
his parents that Mack and Bobby used
to go to you and Mack said you really
got along with Bobby. You should cut
his hair. And his parents say, 'Yeah,
we've got to do something with his
hair. He won't let anyone cut it.'"

They all came in together and
when Bobby saw me he says, "Oscar!
Haircut! Handsome! Handsome!"

So I cut his hair. He was very
happy. I say, "Do you miss your
Grandpa Mack?"

He looked at me and he was
crying. He says, "Mack is gone. Mack
is gone." He cried some more and then
he says, "Okay. I go now."

His parents say, "We've never
seen him cry before."

And they took off. I haven't seen
them since.

The Martini Friendship

My clients were coming in saying, "When are they going to open the new restaurant around the corner?"

I say, "I don't know, man. I guess they're gonna open it soon." My customers know I talk to a lot of people. I told Helene, "Let's take a ride with bicycles and see the restaurant."

So we go to the restaurant and I'm trying to peek in, to see what's going on inside and I'm wearing a tank top, shorts and a hat. So here this guy comes to the door. Blond, beautiful hair, with a martini in his hand. He opens the door and says, "Can I help you?"

I say, "I'm a barber, right down the street from here and all my clients are asking when is this restaurant going to open and I say, 'I'll go check it out and tell you guys.'"

He says to me, "Are you the mayor of the town?"

I say, "No, but everybody comes to me for what's going on in town. They ask me."

He says, "Cool."

I say, "So you like martinis?"

He says, "Yeah. I like a martini, shaken well, with three blue cheese olives."

I say, "Wow. I like it exactly the way you like it."

He says, "Once this place is open, I'd like you and your friend to come in and have a martini with me."

I say, "Deal."

He says, "Can you give me your phone number?"

I say, "Sure."

So I hand him one of my cards and I think, He's not gonna do it. He's just making me feel better. His name was James.

Sure enough, I get a phone call from James a week later. He says, "Hey, Oscar, my restaurant is open. Remember that martini promise that I gave you?"

I say, "Yeah."

He says, "You should come in and get a martini at the bar."

I say, "Sure."

So Helene and I, we go to his bar and we're having a martini and I'm looking at these martini glasses. They were very small. You could barely pour one ounce of a martini in those glasses. Helene and I are looking at these little glasses and James says, "Is there a problem?"

I say, "James! When I met you, you had a martini glass in your hand. You said you liked martinis. I do, too. However, these martini glasses are so tiny."

He says to me, "It's the illusion. They're really bigger."

I say, "James, I know about illusions. I cut hair. But a haircut is a haircut and a martini is a martini and this one looks small."

He says, "What do you think?"

I say, "You should get bigger martini glasses."

He says, "You think so?"

I say, "Try it."

He says, "You know what, you're right. I'm gonna get bigger martini glasses. And I'm gonna call you when I do."

And I say, "In the meantime, you should come and get a haircut. We'll get to meet each other."

We left the place and I'm thinking, Maybe I shouldn't have said anything. He's never going to call me.

So here he comes to my shop a few days later and he says, "Beautiful shop." We talk for a bit and he says, "Can I get a haircut?"

I say, "Sure." He gets a cut and at the end of the cut he says, "Hey, by the way, I got the new martini glasses. I'm re-inviting you guys to come to my restaurant again for a martini."

So we went to his restaurant. He had these new martini glasses. Big ones. Everyone was happy. Since then, he's my customer. We call it the Martini Friendship. Now I get all his business partners for haircuts and his customers get bigger martinis.

The Man Nobody Knew

Jose wasn't this man's real name, but everyone knew him as Jose. We had this little raffle in my shop and I promised I would take my winning customer to this really good restaurant. We had reservations. On the way there, we passed another restaurant, with about a hundred people waiting outside. My customer says, "Damn! I wish we were going to that restaurant."

I say, "You wanna go there?"

The customer says, "Yes, but they don't take reservations."

I say, "If you want to go, that's where you'll go."

So I made a U-turn. I was driving a big SUV. As soon as I pull up, the valet guy comes out. I get out of the car, I take my keys out and he's looking at me like, Who's this guy?

I knew I had to make an impression to get in this place. So I take my keys and throw them at the valet. He's not even asking, do you need a ticket? I made such an impression. I go to the reception desk and say, "I need a table for five."

The guy says, "Are we expecting

you? There's gonna be a wait for a table."

I say, "Do I look like a guy who likes to wait for a table?"

He doesn't know what to say.

I say, "I'm going to be sitting in that bar and within 20 minutes, I'm expecting a table. You got that?"

No answer. We go sit at the bar. We have a couple of drinks and we decide to order some food. The receptionist comes in and says, "Your table is ready."

I say, "You know what? I don't want the table. We've decided to sit in the bar and eat."

So we sit down, we have a great time, we leave the restaurant.

Next day, I'm in the shop cutting hair, I see this very, very dark skinny guy with a white T-shirt walking by with his dry cleaning in his hand. We kind of had eye contact. He's walking and then he slows down, he's turning the corner, and he comes to my shop and he looks and he stops. And I turn my head and he's looking at me.

He comes back slowly and he opens the door. "Excuse me, my brother," he says. "Were you at the restaurant the other night?"

I say, "What restaurant?"

He gave the name and I say, "Yes!"

He says, "Wow! You puzzled us for three days. We were trying to figure out who the fuck you were."

I say, "Excuse me?"

He says, "My boss was saying, 'You guys didn't fuckin' know who he was? You shoulda done better.' Nobody could come up with who this guy was. I'm a waiter there. Jose."

I say, "Nice to meet you. I'm Oscar the Barber."

He says, "Man, you are so cool. I want to get my hair cut by you from now on. Is that okay?"

I say, "Sure."

He says, "I'm going to come every other Thursday at 10 a.m."

I say, "Are you sure?"

He says, "I want to come and get my haircut with you, my brother."

So we started this long relationship, Jose and me. I started going to the restaurant more often. He started coming to me for haircuts more often. He used to have at least $3,000 to $4,000 in his pocket, no ID, nothing. He used to wear cowboy boots pulled over his skinny tight jeans. He had two earrings and pitch-black dyed hair. He was from Mexico. He would go to a suntanning bed. Three times a week!

I'd say, "Jose, why do you go sun tanning? You're already dark."

He says, "I wanna be darker. I wanna be super-dark."

For years and years, we continue our relationship, and he came in every two weeks. One week he comes in and says, "My brother, I want you to have one of my timepieces." He never called them watches. They were timepieces.

I say, "Jose, why do I need a timepiece from you? I have a watch."

He says, "Oscar, you've been a very special friend all these years for me. And I want you to have something from me. Because I'm retiring."

"Retiring?"

"Yes. I'm going to Acapulco. I've got plenty of money. I have plenty of real estate. My parents are super-rich. My condo, my motorcycle, the watches, I want to give everything away."

I found out later on he gave away his stereo, and his beautiful motorcycle. He was a very eccentric guy. He always wore a white T-shirt, but three times a day he changed that shirt. He was very particular. And he was a very good waiter.

So he started giving everything away. As immersed as I was in his friendship, I could never pull anything out of him about his family. He'd say, "Some things are better off left alone."

Interestingly, he never liked gay people. He never liked black people. He didn't like Muslim people either and I say, "I'm Muslim." He'd say, "Oh, you're different." He was never rude but around me he'd make remarks and call them names. It didn't make sense, what he says and what he does.

I get a phone call from a customer who worked with Jose. He says, "Hey, Oscar, do you know what happened to Jose?"

I say, "No, what happened?"

He says, "They found him dead in Birch State Park. Shot in the head. He killed himself with his own gun." He left a note that he'd killed himself and there was nobody to blame.

"Oh, my," I say. "I can't believe that.

He says, "Nobody can believe it,"

I say, "Wow. I'm devastated. Is there going to be a funeral service?"

I'm thinking, Why would he kill himself? He was gonna retire.

I go to the service. It was in Wilton Manors in a church with mostly gay people, which was very interesting because I knew how he felt about gays. Why Wilton Manors? Half the room was African-American. That was interesting, knowing he didn't like black people. During the service many people came up and talked about him and how they knew him, what he was all about, and everybody had a different story and everybody had a different perspective of Jose.

I was shocked, sitting at his funeral, looking at and listening to these people. They were talking about fifty different personalities in this one person.

Later on, I did a lot of digging on Jose's story. I wanted to know what really happened. He used to try to make me believe he was a drug lord in Acapulco and he had to give everything away to leave there. I never really believed that.

I heard that he was in the US illegally and he was using someone else's driver's license and Social Security number and somehow, the driver's license office found out, so he couldn't get another driver's license. He had no documentation. He freaked out about it.

I heard from other people that he was actually gay and he couldn't come out.

I heard all sorts of things: That he was a big porn star in Germany. That he was a big swinger and he might have done something that was going to cause trouble. Today, I still don't know his first name. Nobody knows the truth of Jose's story. Except Jose himself.

He died a mystery. However, he will always be "my brother."

The Man Who Had One Beer

I worked with David, he was slow, not real bright. He had a drinking and drug problem. He had long dark hair. He loved Mickey Mouse and characters like that. He acted like he was 13 years old. He comes to work one day and he says, "Oscar, I'm going to have to go to court tomorrow."

I say, "What happened?"

He says, "I had a DUI over the weekend. I was arrested."

I say, "That's a big deal."

But he was a little slow and he didn't sound like it was a big deal for him, even if it was. I say, "Take tomorrow off."

Early the next morning, the salon gets a call. Someone gives me the phone and says, "Oscar, there's a cop on the phone."

I say, "A cop?"

"Yeah."

So the cop says, "Hi, is this Oscar? I've got your friend David here. I stopped him."

I say, "Why did you stop him?"

The cop says, "Your friend says he's on his way to go to DUI court for the first appearance."

I say, "Yes."

The cop says, "It's interesting why I stopped him. He was drinking beer in his car at a red light."

I say, "WHAT?"

The cop says, "Yeah. I stopped him right near the courthouse and asked for his driver's license and registration and before he grabs it he takes a sip of this cold beer. And I say, 'What the hell do you think you're doing?' He says, 'Drinking beer.' The cop says to him, 'BEER! You're not supposed to drink beer.' The guy says, 'I only had one beer.' The cop says, 'No! You can't do that!'"

I say, "Officer, he's not a hundred percent there."

The cop says, "No shit. I can see that. Who drinks beer on the way to a DUI appearance?"

The cop says, "I told him, 'I don't understand what's going on here' and your friend says, 'Call Oscar. He'll explain.'"

So I say, "I think in his mind he thinks it's okay to drink one beer and drive. The beer calms him down."

The cop says to David, "Your friend says the beer calms you down."

David says, "See? Oscar knows. Talk to him. Talk to him more."

I say, "Officer, we've worked together for a while. As you can see, he's not good at thinking. Can you do something for him?"

The officer says, "I don't know what to do. He's drinking beer. I could write him up and he'd lose his license forever."

I say, "If he loses his license, he won't be able to come to work. I don't know what will happen to him."

The cop says, "Does he have any family?"

I say, "Nope."

The cop says to David, "Okay, give me your keys. We're going to park your car right here. Take whatever you think is valuable. Just go to the courtroom. Think of today as Christmas Day."

David tells the cop, "Oh, thank you so much. I'll go right now. I don't want to be late."

The cops says to me, "Guess what he's trying to take out of the back of his trunk?"

I say, "What?"

The cop says, "A case of beer! Should I put him in jail or a mental institution?"

The cop says to me, "Dude, I'm going to get off the phone. Tell your friend not to drink and drive. Not that I think he'll listen. But he needs some help."

I get David on the phone and say, "David, drop the fucking beer."

He says, "But Oscar, I only had one beer."

The Macho Man

Lou was unique. He looked like Al Pacino. Same haircut, same eyes, same face. He was Italian. But he's got these two little dogs in his arms. He used to walk around with them. He'd bring them to the shop.

He was rude. He could go from a perfectly nice gentleman to an asshole in milliseconds. I'm doing this charity benefit and I'm auctioning off this $50 shampoo basket. Everybody's bidding on the basket. He comes to me and he says, "Oscar, you know I'm gonna win it. I'll give you 200 bucks. I'll take it home now."

I say, "Lou, I can't do that. Other people want to bid on it."

Lou says, "What's the point? I never lose."

I'm in the barber shop and I say, "Okay, everybody, we're going to auction this basket off for charity now. What do you want to pay for it?"

This guy says, "50 bucks!"

Lou says, "A hundred bucks."

The first guy says, "$125."

Lou says, "200."

The guy says, "225."

Lou gets up and says, "Look,

man, I got a whole lot more money than you do. I'm taking this basket home."

The guy says, "$300."

Lou gets out of the chair with the two dogs and says, "Oh, you wanna play that game? You wanna play that game? We're gonna play that game. Okay, 500!"

I say, "Lou, this is dumb. This is like $50 in shampoo."

He says, "Oscar, get out of my way."

The other guy gets up and he says, "550."

Lou says, "750 bucks and you open your mouth, I'm gonna say a thousand bucks."

The guy looks at me and then says, "Take the basket home."

So Lou grabs the basket and he says to the guy, "I told you I was gonna get it."

He says to me, "Oscar, I want to take you out to dinner tonight to celebrate. We're going to go to this very good Italian restaurant." I know the restaurant. It's really expensive and really crowded.

I say, "Lou, it's Saturday night. How are we going to get in? We're not even dressed up."

He says, "We'll go to my place and get some clothes. Don't worry about it."

I say, "We don't have reservations. We can't go into this place."

He says, "I'm so excited I won this basket I want to celebrate it."

I'm like, "Okay, Lou."

We go to his place, and just like Al Pacino, he combs his hair – wet hair, changes his shirt, puts on a jacket, then we go to the restaurant.

I'm thinking there's no freaking way we're gonna get into this place. He's gonna get upset and things are gonna turn ugly. The restaurant is small and narrow. People are seated on top of one another. It's packed!

Here comes the owner. He separates people with his arms. Lou comes in and they start hugging each other and talking. I'm right behind him. The owner says, "You guys having dinner?"

I look at Lou. He says, "What do you think we're gonna do? Of course we're having dinner."

The owner says, "Okay, give me two seconds."

Lou says, "See, I told you. No problem."

I see this waiter, just like in the movies. He puts a table upside down on his head. I know it's our table. I'm looking at it and wondering where the hell is he gonna put this table.

He puts it in the middle of the other tables. It's literally touching people's chairs. And two other waiters are pushing people to move down, saying "Excuse me, excuse me." People are like, "What's going on?"

These people are all pushed together and they made room for us, right in the middle of the restaurant.

I am like, Wow! I have never been impressed so much.

The waiter says, "Would you like something to drink?"

I'm like, "Lou, this is gonna cost a lot of money."

Lou says, "Don't worry about it."

He ordered an expensive wine. We had a great meal and I say, "How did you do this? Why would the restaurant owner do this for you?"

He says, "Oscar: loyalty and friendship and honesty and integrity. Those are very important things in life. You keep these things in life and you will always have friends and friends will always know who you are.

"That's how I got this table."

That was a lovely thought.

Then I found out later the restaurant owner's father knew Lou's father. They were lifelong friends.

The Sick Man

This guy was a big, heavy dude from New York. He says, "Hey, can I ask you a question?"

I'm like, "Yeah."

He says, "Do you know where I can get my shoes shined?"

I say, "A shoe shine?"

He says, "Yeah, some barber shops have a shoe shine. You guys do that?"

I say, "No, man. You're in Florida. Everybody's got sandals. Nobody wears shined shoes."

He says, "Can you recommend some place?"

I say, "You can get one of those things online to shine your shoes."

He says, "No, I want it by hand. It has to be by hand."

I say, "There's a place in Coral Ridge Mall. A shoe repair place. You can go there."

He comes back a week or two later and says, "Kid, you were right. I got my shoes shined."

I say, "Great."

He says, "Can I come and get a haircut?"

I cut his hair for years. He didn't

have much hair.

His name was Moe. When Moe called you on the phone, he wanted you to drop everything and listen to him.

Moe calls one day and says, "Hey, can I get a haircut?"

I say, "Moe, I really don't have much time to talk. When do you want to come in? What day and time?"

He says, "Never mind," and *click!* He hangs up on me. I'm so busy. I can't stop the world and take care of Moe. That night, I feel bad. I text him. "Hey, Moe, what's going on? You want to come tomorrow?"

No answer.

Next morning, I send him another text message, "Moe, what's going on?"

No answer.

I think, You know what? He doesn't respect me. I don't respect him.

Two weeks later, I'm still thinking about Moe. I liked this guy. A big New York teddy bear.

He comes in two weeks later and says, "Oscar, I felt like I was being treated like the new kid on the block. I don't appreciate the way you talked to me. I've already found another barber."

That's it. I give him my standard Dear John letter. I say, "Moe, I feel so bad that you feel that way. I thought we had a stronger relationship. I still think you're a cool guy. Sometimes relationships have a shelf life. We've reached the end of ours. I wish you all the best."

He says, "Oscar, you will always be my friend and I'll always see you as my friend. Hope it doesn't change our friendship."

I'm like, "Sure, Moe." He's an old man. I don't want to hurt his feelings.

A couple months later I see Moe and he's going into the post office in our shopping center – our shop is very close to the post office – and I'm driving my car. He almost fell. And his wife came out of the car, running. Moe was a big guy. His wife was a small woman. She could barely hold onto him.

I jump out of my car, afraid this big dude is gonna fall and hit his head on the concrete. He kept shaking his head, No, no, I don't want you to come near me.

He looked at me with eye

contact and says, "No!"

I like raise my hands and say, "No problem." His wife never saw me. I got back into my car, he held onto something, and I let it go.

I was saying to myself, What an asshole! He hated me that much?

I went home and talked about it with my friend, saying "I don't believe this guy. He wouldn't let me help him. I knew him for years and years."

A couple of his friends came to me for haircuts. One says, "Hey, Moe is very sick and he's in the hospital."

I say, "Wow, I feel so bad. I saw him the other day and I tried to help him and he looked at me and he shook his head no."

His friend says, "I know, Oscar. He was so upset that he was sick. He didn't have the guts to tell you good-bye."

Later on, he died. His wife called me and said, "Oscar, Moe always said you were the best barber he ever had. He never wanted to become a dead customer of yours. He wanted to break up with you before he was forced to be broken up."

The Famous Chef

I get a call from this agency. They say, "We have a very famous chef," and they give me his name. You would know it. Everyone knows it. The agency says, "He's opening a restaurant tonight in Fort Lauderdale and he wants to look presentable. Can you take care of his hair?"

"Absolutely!" I say.

Here this guy comes in, a good-looking guy. He comes with his mom. I cut his hair and I'm like, "Dude, you're opening a restaurant tonight."

He says, "Yeah, I'm very excited."

I know where he's opening the restaurant. I say, "Wow, that's great. I'm very honored that you come to me for a haircut."

He says, "Funny you brought that up. I don't even know where the restaurant is."

I say, "What do you mean, you don't know? You're opening a restaurant and you don't know where it is?"

He says, "Yeah. I open multiple restaurants. People send me pictures, videos, plans, this and that. I know *where* it is, but I haven't been there."

So his mom says, "You've heard about him opening the restaurant?"

I say, "Yeah."

She says, "Why don't you take us to the restaurant tonight? And show us where it is."

I said, "I'll take you guys there, but it's in a hotel. Aren't you staying at the hotel?"

She says, "You're such a lovely guy. Why don't you take us to the restaurant, show us where it is, and then come back tonight, as our guest?"

So we went there, we had dinner there, the food was good, everything was great. A week later, the chef comes back. I say, "I just cut your hair. Everything OK at the restaurant?"

He says, "Yeah, everything is okay, but I don't like the location of the restaurant. I just wanted to come in and say good-bye to you."

I say, "Good-bye? You haven't even been here for one week."

He says, "I have other plans I want to pursue. I thought that you would be great, you have this terrific personality, you should run this restaurant for me."

I say, "Me! What would I do at a

restaurant?"

He says, "I sat down with my mom, all night long we talked about it, all the investment, the money in that restaurant, and my mom says, 'How about that guy who cut your hair? He'd be good at running it.'"

I say, "Is this a joke?"

He says, "No, no, my mom and I, we sat down and talked, and we think you'd be great. I promise I'll give you an allowance, you can get yourself nice suits, you'll make sure the restaurant is running properly."

I'm thinking, Is this guy real?

The chef says, "No, no, I'm for real. If you say yes, I'll have my lawyers get in touch with you and it could be an adventure. From time to time we'll keep in touch. I don't like to come here but my mom loves you."

I say, "I'm a barber. I cut hair. What do I know about running a restaurant?"

He says, "I can accept that. I kinda told my mom, 'Mom, don't make me go over there and talk to this guy.' My mom said, 'But he's so cute!'"

Being cute doesn't run a business.

The Hollywood Big Deal

So this big Hollywood actor-producer's mother used to come into the shop. She has a condo here. One day, I'm outside, hanging around the shop. When it's quiet, I go out, talk to the neighbors. I see this guy with a hat sitting outside.

I say to him, "Hey, how you doing?"

He says, "Hey man, I'm fine."

I say, "Dude, your hair is pretty long. It's coming out of your hat. How about a haircut?"

He says, "You wanna cut my hair?"

I say, "Yeah, I wanna cut your hair."

He says, "Why would you wanna cut my hair?"

I say, "I don't have a customer. You seem like a cool guy and you're obviously waiting for someone to get their hair done."

He looks at me like, Seriously?

I say, "Dude, don't be nervous. It's just a haircut." I had no idea who he was.

So we go inside, I wash his hair, nobody looked at him twice. I sit him down and start cutting his hair. He says, "You've got a good personality. You came out and started talking to me. I guess you don't lack for business."

I say, "When I don't have business, I create it. You're sitting in my chair, getting your hair cut."

I say, "Where are you from?"

He says, "I reside in California."

I say, "California, where the cool people hang out. What do you do out there? Don't tell me you're in the movie business."

He says, "I'm kinda in the movie business."

I say, "What do you do? Commercial movies and stuff?"

He says, "I shoot some movies, I direct some movies."

I say, "No shit. Any movies I would know?"

He says, "You watch a lot of movies?"

I say, "Once a week, I go see a movie."

He tells me the name of a movie – I don't remember it. I looked at him twice and say, "Oh, shit. Are you —?"

He says, "Yes, I am. And I want you to keep it quiet."

I say, "Sure, I'll keep it quiet."

So I cut his hair. He was a very cool guy. I met his kids. I met his mother. He said one of the things he gets a kick out of is when he talks to people and they don't know who he is. He brings the conversation to himself and starts asking questions. He says, "When I looked at you and started talking to you, I knew you had no idea who I was. It's such a pleasure. I live for that feeling. Thank you so much for making me feel that way."

I say, "No problem." Also, no tip. He didn't tip me a dime.

The Philly Cheese Steak

Luca was an Italian guy. He comes to my shop and the first thing he says is, "Let me tell you something."

I say, "What?"

He says, "You know how to make a Philly cheese steak?"

I say, "No."

He says, "You get the steak, you shave it very, very thin. I get the steak from an Italian guy. You can't get it. Even if you wanted to get it, you can't get it because I get it.

"Then you get a little bit of Parmesan and you take it and chop it fine, fine, fine. Three times, right?"

He would tell you how to make a Philly cheese steak and he was a very funny guy.

He had a wife named Maria. Luca is in his late sixties, very macho Italian guy. His wife was from Colombia. She was drop-dead gorgeous.

He used to get his hair colored and highlighted and he'd get a really cool haircut. It didn't match his personality at all.

He'd say, "Oscar, when I come in

I want you to do everything."

He was so jealous of his wife.
He used to tell me how he met his
wife. He went to Colombia and he
walked into a restaurant because he
saw her. She was sitting with this
group of drug lords. He walked up to
one drug lord and said, "Just tell me
the number you want but I want her
to come with me."

The drug lord says, "Wow. I've
never met anyone so brave like you.
When you came in here by yourself, a
gringo, we thought you were crazy.
You're crazier than me. Here she is.
Take her with you."

Luca takes her to the United
States. She didn't speak one word of
English.

I found out he was in charge of a
big union. People say he was the real
deal. So one day when he came in for
a haircut I say, "Luca, let me ask you
something. People are saying you're
like a wise guy."

He says, "Oscar, I never want to
hear this. Wise guys used to come to
my union. They used to wanna tax
me. And I'd say, 'What are you fuckin'
talking about? Nobody taxes Luca!'
Only one who taxes me is her" – and

he pointed to his wife. "I used to take my baseball bat and chase them away and say, 'Don't you ever come back in here!'"

His wife used to come in when he got a haircut. She'd wait for him. She wasn't allowed to get her nails done. She wasn't allowed to get anything done. She used to just sit there.

He'd say, "Hey! Is it cold in here?"

I'd say, "I'm fine."

He'd say, "It's cold!" He'd take off his cape and put it around his wife. And I'd say, "Luca! That thing's got hair all over it. I can give her something clean."

He'd say, "No, no, no. This is fine." He'd wrap her up. I'd put another cape on him and say, "Luca, stop doing this."

She had learned English by this time and she'd say, "Luca, don't do this."

One day he says, "I got a new Mercedes. It's red. But it's not a regular red. It's Mars red."

I say, "What's a Mars red?"

He says, "Come outside and I'll show it to you." So I did. He says, "If you get a Mercedes, it has to be Mars red."

He says, "If I see you get a Mercedes and it's not Mars red, I'm not going to like it."

I say, "Luca, I'm not going to get a Mercedes. I can't afford it."

He says, "Okay, but if you ever get a Mercedes, it has to be Mars red."

I say, "Okay."

I have friends, they have cars. We travel around. They pick me up. I never heard from Luca again after the car incident. So I call him up. "Luca, I haven't heard from you. Where have you been?"

He says, "Oscar, I'm going to be honest with you. I think you have a Mercedes."

I'm like, "I don't have a Mercedes."

He says, "I think you have a Mercedes and I think it's not Mars red. I told you if you ever get a Mercedes you should get a Mars red one and I saw you in a gray Mercedes."

He says, "I have to be honest. I got hurt. You looked at me and said, 'Luca, if I ever get a Mercedes it's gonna be Mars red.'"

I say, "Luca, it's not even my

Mercedes. That's my friend Sam's car. You don't have to get agitated like this."

He disappeared. I've never seen him again. No one has. Whenever I run into someone who knew him they say, "Let me tell you something. You know how to make a Philly cheese steak?" Then we both start laughing.

The Man with Four Daughters

As soon as I met Sam, we clicked. He had white hair, he used to color it black, jet black. He had a nice, beautiful mustache, he would keep it white. He had four daughters and no sons, and he was really upset about this. He came from a culture where a man had to have sons. I'm not saying he didn't love his daughters, but his life would have been complete with sons.

He'd come in upset and I'd say, "What's the matter?"

He'd say, "My daughter is dating this douche bag and I'm fuckin' upset. I'm thinking. 'Is he the fuckin' one who's gonna take all my money?'"

I'd say, "What do you mean?"

He says, "Oscar, I have four daughters. I have the first one and I say, 'Hey, doc, do you think the next one is gonna be a boy?'

"The doctor says, 'I don't know, Sam. There's a 50-50 chance.' So I say to my wife, 'We should have another kid.' It's another daughter. I go to the doctor again, I say, 'Doctor, should we have another kid?' The doctor says,

'Well, when you have two daughters, the odds are you'll have a boy next.' I come home and say to my wife, 'We should have another kid.' So we do and I get another daughter. Now we have three of them. So I say to the doctor, 'Doc, what is the chance of this baby – the fourth – being a boy?' The doctor says, 'Well, most likely, it's going to be a boy.' But guess what? I end up with another daughter. The doctor says, 'Hey, Sam, I think the fifth one will be a boy.'

"Sam says to him, 'Fuck you, I'm changing doctors. I have four daughters now.'"

He's built this empire. He's got five floors in a very expensive condo. The top five floors. He lives on top and he's got four daughters living underneath with their boyfriends or husbands or whatever.

One day, he comes into the shop and says, "Oscar, I've got the answer to my problem."

I say, "What?"

He says, "Oscar, just pick one of my girls. Just pick one of them. I really like you. If my money is going to go to someone, it should go to you."

I say, "Sam, I'm married. I've got

my life and everything."

I turned him down. I turned down a fortune – not that any of his daughters would have married me.

The Treasure Hunter

One of my customers, Larry, he's a crane operator. When he first came into my shop, he wore shorts and his socks very high, and super, super shiny shoes. He's a very eccentric guy. A tall guy, very well-spoken.

The first time he says, "Hi, sir, my name is Larry. I've heard a lot about you. I really appreciate you taking the time to cut my hair."

I thought, That's flattering.

I cut his hair and he says, "That's it! I'm never going to go anywhere else. You've cut my hair exactly the way I want it. I've been to ten different people and I wasn't happy."

I found out when he was a crane operator he'd helped build most of the US embassies around the world. He's been to every place you can think of – the Middle East, Russia, Europe. For 30 years, he worked for the US government. He made a lot of money. Crane operators can make between $200,000 and $300,000. He worked in the ruins of 9/11. He's a very knowledgeable guy.

But he's very simple. He likes to drive a BMW, nothing fancy. It's like a

30-year-old BMW, but kept in good shape and he doesn't believe in trading it in because he likes it.

He got into treasure hunting. He's got super-rich friends. They live in $50-$60,000,000 houses. He shows me pictures of him with them and he still drives his old BMW. He says to one friend, "Hey, you know that island you own?"

His friend says, "Yeah." This guy owns an island.

Larry says, "I've been reading about your island and there are a lot of ships sunk around your island and I think there's treasure around there."

His friend says, "Larry, I don't care. I don't know anything about it."

Larry says, "Would you allow me to do a bit of digging?"

The friend says, "Sure, if you want to. But please don't tell anybody."

Larry says to me, "Well, Oscar, I found something."

I say, "What did you find?"

He says, "I found a cannon."

"A cannon?"

He says, "Yeah."

I say, "Wow, that's very interesting."

He says, "Would you like to see it?"

I say, "Where is the cannon?"

He says, "It's in my trunk."

I say, "You have a cannon in your trunk?"

So we go outside and he opens his trunk, and there's this big cannon. He says, "This is from the 1400s. It's going to be part of a museum. I showed it to you because I know how much interest you had in this project."

I say, "Larry, I feel bad that you dragged this cannon all the way here."

He says, "I'm a man of my word. I promised I'd follow up with you."

I say, "How much is something like this worth, do you think?"

He says, "Probably $150,000."

I say, "This is $150,000? You are going to be a rich man."

He says, "Oh, no. I told my friend who owned the island I don't want any money. This is all going to a museum."

I say, "You are on this island, treasure hunting, finding these things,

and you don't want any money out of it?"

"No," he says. "The pleasure I get

out of finding treasure is priceless.
That's what I was looking for and
that's what I found."

The US Marshal

I had this Italian guy who used to come to me. A neat guy. He had salt-and-pepper hair. He was in his 70s. He always acted like he was a wise guy, but he wasn't a wise guy. I found out he was a US marshal. Once I found out he was a US marshal, we started talking about his stories, about how he used to go to South America, knock down doors, get these drug dealers. His name was Nick.

I'd say, "Nick, weren't you scared of these drug dealers?"

He'd say, "Oh, no, I had my crew. There were six of us. I would bet my mom's life on these guys I used to hang out with."

One Saturday, late in the afternoon, Nick was inside the shop, waiting to get a haircut. He was next, as soon as I finished the customer I was working on.

This bunch of young guys came in the shop. They were big, masculine guys, and they were drunk. There were three or four them, in their 20s. They'd spent a lot of time at the beach and they wanted haircuts. They didn't speak much English. They're trying to get haircuts and Nick tries to explain to them. He tells them, "Hey, man, it's my turn."

They were shaking their heads no. They were getting agitated. I'm looking at the whole situation, I'm trying to finish my customer, and I'm wondering what's going to happen.

Next thing I know, my customer gets up, he goes to the register and I'm cashing him out. One of the boys sits right in my chair. And he's like, "All right, man, cut me. Cut me. I gotta go."

I'm trying to explain to him, "Dude, it's not your turn. You gotta wait."

Nick calmly went to the guy and he says, "Hey! One time. Get out of the chair. Exit the chair."

I say, "Nick, I don't think they speak the language. I don't think they understand."

He says, "Oscar, trust me. Everybody understands 'Get the fuck out' and 'Exit.' I've been all over the world as a US marshal. I know how this works."

This kid says to Nick, "Fuck you!" with an accent.

Nick hit him so hard, he

punched him right out. This 70-year-old man, who must weigh about 150 pounds, he punched the kid so fast, so quick, he knocked him out sitting in the chair. The kid passed out.

It happened so quick his three friends didn't even know their friend had been punched out.

I'm watching this. I've never seen anyone knocked out so quick. Nick looked at me like, Don't make any moves. Calm down. Relax.

I was nervous. I thought, Now there's going to be a big brawl.

Nick goes to the other guys and he tries to explain to them. He puts his arms around their shoulders and says, "Hey, your friend is so drunk, he fell asleep."

They picked up their friend – literally – and dragged him out the door. Two are holding him while one opens the door. They never questioned what Nick told them.

Nick says, "All right. Let's cut my hair. I've got a date tonight."

Another time – I'm not a gambler, I hate gambling – but for some reason I'm at the Hard Rock Casino. I see Nick in line, talking with three or four other guys. I don't know

if they're cops or wise guys or what.
They're in line to cash out or
something.

This one guy behind Nick, a big
guy, says, "Hey, Pops, why don't you
move on. You're holding up the line.

Nick says, "Hey, buddy, I'm
gonna talk to this guy one more
second and then I'm moving on. I'm
not holding up the line."

The big guy says, "Hey, Pops,
I'm not gonna tell you twice. MOVE or
I'm gonna make you move."

BAM! Nick hits him. He hits him
so hard that the big guy is on the
ground. He had two or three friends
standing with him. And they're like,
"What the fuck? What happened?"

Nick says to me, "I gotta run."
And he takes off running. I'm there
with the friends of the guy who got
punched and I'm wondering, Are they
gonna attack me?

The guys are looking at me. I'm
looking at them. Some people start
screaming and security comes. "What
happened?" security asks.

I say, "I don't know what
happened. I was standing in line. Next
thing I know, this guy just dropped."

I wanted out of there. I walked

to my car. I couldn't believe I'd seen
the same scenario twice. There's Nick
outside the casino, just having a
cigarette. He says, "Oscar, where you
been? I've been waiting for you. You
gotta give me a ride."

Now I believed all his stories
about being a marshal.

He passed away, unfortunately.
Cancer got him. He came in before he
died and he looked bad. He was
clearly dying. He says, "You've seen
my good times, you've seen my bad
times. Now it's over. They're gonna
give me some fucked up haircut for
my coffin. I'll keep coming to you
until I die."

I say, "Nick, you look like shit.
I'm gonna be honest."

He says, "I know. Thanks for the
honesty."

I cut his hair, and a week later,
he passed away. I went to his funeral.
He'd left a note: "Don't cut my hair.
Oscar's cut it already."

The Crooked Lawyer

I had this client, a big-shot lawyer. You'd know his name if I told you. Everyone in the US knows his name. He used to come to me for haircuts.

When I first met the lawyer, I turn to my friend in the salon and say, "This guy's a crook."

My friend says, "What are you talking about? He's a very famous lawyer. Has a huge firm."

I say, "He's got a driver. Name me a lawyer you know who has a driver. Name one."

My friend says, "Yeah, you got a point."

I liked to go to this nice restaurant and every time I'd go there, I'd see the lawyer there. He used to buy me a $300 bottle of wine. I'd tell the waiter, Billy, "I don't want it."

Billy would say, "Oscar, just take the wine. He doesn't care if you want it or not. He runs a tab in here."

I used to joke with Billy, "This guy is gonna get locked up. And when it does happen, it's gonna happen here."

The staff used to laugh at me

and say, "Oh, Oscar, stop talking shit like that. He'll sue you or something."

I say, "Nah. He's my client. I know the man."

The lawyer used to come for haircuts and we'd talk to each other. He always had a big presence. You can sometimes tell about insecure people, or people who are doing stuff they're not supposed to do. They cover up their bad conscience with outgoing personalities.

He used to walk in the shop and say, "HEY, HOW YA DOING! WHAT'S GOING ON?"

He wore flashy clothes, like a $6,000 shiny suit. He had a driver and a little entourage with him. He used to come up to the beautiful women in my shop and say, "Hey, Beautiful, you look so gorgeous. I love your top." He used to bring gifts to some of my colleagues. He liked the woman who did the shampooing – he'd give her flowers. He'd even bring flowers for some of the guys.

He'd tell me, "Oscar, you gotta do what you have to do."

I'd say, "Hey, man, as a lawyer, what if someone is guilty and you know it? What would you do if they'd killed someone? Would you represent him?"

He'd say, "Oscar, it's my job. I gotta do what I gotta do."

One day, I' m doing a haircut and my phone rings. It's Billy, one of the guys from the restaurant. I don't pick up. It rings again. I don't pick up again. It rings a third time. It happens a fourth time. I tell my customer, "Something is going on. This guy keeps calling me."

The customer says, "Go for it."

I say to my customer, "I apologize. I don't want to disrupt your cut, but it must be important."

I make the call and hear Billy screaming, "YOU WERE RIGHT! THEY GOT HIM RIGHT HERE. The FBI is in the house, taking his ass out. How did you know?"

I say, "I didn't know. Every time I come to the restaurant, he's there with his entourage, drinking expensive wines, buying dinner for everybody. I have some of the most successful lawyers for clients. Most of them are very low-key people. It doesn't matter how much money they make. I figured if that lawyer got popped, it will be in this restaurant because the FBI is watching his ass, too."

The Millionaire Who Met Madoff

I've got this customer, Milt. He hangs out with me in the shop. I didn't hear from him for a while, so I texted him, "Hey, Milt, what's going on?"

He texts me back, "Oh, Oscar, I've been so busy." He gave me the same excuse a couple of times.

His wife, Sandy, used to come into the shop. She says, "Did you see Milt yet?"

I say, "No, I texted him. He's been really busy, playing golf, doing this, doing that."

"Uh, huh, uh, huh," Sandy says. "You don't know what happened, do you?"

I'm like, "No."

She says, "I'm going to come with him myself. He must be too embarrassed to see you."

I say, "Really? Did anything bad happen?"

She says, "No, no. You talk to Milt. He'll tell you."

A week later, Milt calls. He says, "I hear you ran into my wife in the shop."

I say, "Milt, she's always in here,

getting her hair done, her nails done, and she says you must be too embarrassed to come in. What happened? Did you get a haircut somewhere else?"

He says, "I wish! It's not that. I'll tell you when I come for a cut."

So he comes in with his wife. He and Sandy had worked hard their entire lives. They were so proud of the money they'd made and saved. He used to tell me how to do investments, where I should go, don't spend my money on stupid stuff. He took pride in his investments.

He says, "One day, my friends and I are playing golf, and my friend's wife says to Sandy, 'My husband met this guy in New York. He makes a lot of money for us.'"

"Sandy says, 'How much money?'

"The friend's wife says, 'Oh, so much money. But he doesn't take everybody.'"

"Sandy says, 'We got money.'"

Milt overhears this conversation and says, "What's the deal?"

His friend tells Milt, "His name is Madoff. He makes a lot of money for a lot of people. But, Milt, I have to be honest, he doesn't take most people."

Milt says, "What are you talking about? I've got money. I want my money to be invested with him."

His friend says, "I can get you the phone number, but it's up to him to take you."   Milt looks at me and I say, "Madoff? Really?"

Milt says, "Oscar, it gets even better. I just wanna cry."

I say, "Don't cry. Tell me what happened."

He says, "I make this appointment. Forty-five days. FORTY-FIVE DAYS this guy made me wait to get an appointment with him. Before the appointment, his office calls me and say, 'Sir, you need to be here one hour prior to your appointment so we can go through your investment portfolio. And you only have ten minutes with Mr. Madoff.'

"So I got nervous," Milt says. "Like I'm going to high school or something. I'm excited, too. This guy's making everyone so much money. I researched him. The market guys, even the inspectors are saying how great Madoff is and everything."

I'm saying, "Milt . . ."

He says, "Oscar, please. Please let me finish."

So Milt arrives at Madoff's office on time. It was a gorgeous office with a beautiful receptionist. She says, "I need you to fill out these forms."

So he sits down and fills out the forms and one form asks Milt how much money he wants to invest. Milt tells me, "I don't know how much money I want to invest. I just want to talk to the guy." But he puts down one million dollars. Milt's rich.

He says, "Just because I put down one million dollars, they can't force me to invest a million. I'm very proud. I'm sitting there like I own the office. The receptionist takes the paperwork and three minutes later she comes back and says, 'Excuse me, Mr. Milt. I'm going to have to decline this appointment time that you had with Mr. Madoff. I'm going to have to schedule you with David, and David will take care of all your investment needs.'"

So Milt says to me, "What the fuck? Why is David doing this? So I say to the receptionist, 'I don't want David. I want Madoff.'

"She says, 'Well, unfortunately,

Mr. Madoff doesn't see personal clients unless you want to make an investment of about four million dollars.'"

This is when Milt calls his wife. He says, "I really want to meet this guy. Unless I have four million, I'm not going to meet the guy." Sandy's having tea with her friends. Sandy tells me, "I'm with my girlfriends and this idiot calls me and says he wants to meet Mr. Madoff. The guy says, 'Four million dollars or he doesn't want to see me. What do you want me to do?'"

So Sandy says, "You're a smart man. Do what you gotta do, Milt." She hangs up.

I say to her, "Why didn't you say to him, 'Milt, don't do it?'"

Sandy says, "Because later he would have said to me, 'Why didn't you let me do it?'"

Milt tells the receptionist, "I wanted to put down 14 million dollars, not four." He puts down 14 million.

The receptionist says, "Mr. Milt, that's what I figured, but I didn't want to insult you."

Milt's thinking, Shit! I don't even

have ten million!

I say to him, "Milt, why?"

He says, "I don't know, Oscar. I wanted to meet the guy."

The receptionist says, "Just sit tight, Mr. Milt, and you're going to go in."

So he did. Madoff was well-dressed, well-spoken. He gets up to greet Milt. He says, "I looked at your portfolio. You seem to meet our criteria. I will get you as much of a return as I can. Your money's at the best place, you don't have to worry about it. With 14 million dollars, I can get you a good return."

Milt says, "Mr. Madoff, I gotta come clean. I don't have 14 million dollars."

Madoff says, "Then why did you put 14 million in your application?"

Milt says, "I put one million and they say I gotta meet David. I don't wanna meet David. I wanna meet Madoff. I called my wife and she says, 'Do what you gotta do.'"

Madoff says, "Smart wife."

Milt says, "Yeah. My wife is really smart."

Madoff says, "Mr. Milt, how much money do you really have?"

Milt says, "I'm not exactly sure."

Madoff says, "I'll tell you what. I don't usually do this. However, I like you."

Milt says to me, "Oscar, when he fuckin' said, 'I don't usually do this. However, I like you,' I knew I was getting fucked. Then Madoff says, 'Why don't you take the office we have for private clients at the end of the hall? Make some phone calls and find out how much you really can invest.' Two girls come in and escort me down the hall. They say, 'Do you want whiskey?' I'm on a high floor and I'm looking outside at all these buildings. I'm feeling on top the world.

"I call my wife and she asks what happened. I tell her Madoff really likes me. He doesn't usually do this for clients. Sandy says, 'You know what they say on the street, Milt? If you think you're getting fucked, you're getting fucked.'"

Milt tells her all the reasons why this is a good idea. Then he makes some phone calls and gathers all his money and sees Madoff. Madoff tells him, "Well, this is not a typical deal, but I like you. I'll take it."

A year after that, Madoff was busted. Milt and Sandy lost all their money. Except for $250,000.

I say, "Milt, you lost it all?"

He says, "I lost it all. Thank God for my sons. They're the ones taking care of us now."

I say, "Didn't you say to yourself, 'Let me keep a little bit in a checking account?'"

Milt says, "When Madoff said to me, 'I don't usually do this. However, I like you' I said to myself, Either you're getting fucked all the way, or this will be huge. They made me feel like a king. So I did it."

The Man with Someone Else's Lungs

I had one guy, white hair. He comes in the shop and he's wearing a white T-shirt. It says: "These Lungs Are Not Mine."

It's an odd T-shirt for a big man to be wearing. He sits down, he's getting a haircut and I quickly realize he's from Canada. I put the cape on him and say, "Nice T-shirt you've got."

He says, "You like it? I made that T-shirt."

I say, "Why would you say these lungs are not yours? Do you smoke cigarettes?"

He says, "I smoked for 30 years, but not any more."

I say, "What happened?"

He says, "You wanna see why?" He takes his shirt off. He had a big scar, all the way down his chest. He'd had a double lung transplant.

"Whoa!" I say. "Dude, I have never met anyone in my life with a double lung transplant."

He puts his shirt back on. He says, "Me, too.

"People tell me that all the time. I'd been smoking for years and I went to the doctor one day and he says, 'Your lungs are so bad. You're gonna die. You need to get new lungs.'

"My wife was there and I say to her, 'Go get me some lungs from the grocery story.'

"We were joking about it and three months later, I can't breathe, and they put these lungs in. Now I'm breathing. I'm feeling great. Since then, I made these T-shirts. They say, 'These Lungs Are Not Mine.' People say, 'Nice T-shirt. What's with it?' I lift up my T-shirt and I show them. And they say, 'Whoa! I've never met anyone with a double lung transplant' and I say, 'Me, too.'"

The Man with the Bag of Money

This guy comes in and asks, "How much is a haircut?"

I tell him and he says, "That sounds good. I'll come in tomorrow."

I take his phone number. He says he lives across the street. There's a lot of big houses over there.

He comes in. I start cutting his hair. We start talking about money and investments. I realize he's a stockbroker. He's been doing this for a long time.

I asked him why he chose this shop and he says, "Oh, this is a fun place. I like coming in here."

As he gets ready to pay, he says, "Oh, shoot. I don't have any cash on me."

I say, "That's okay. Bring it later."

He says, "No, no. I feel terrible. I have a golf cart outside. I can take you to my house in my golf cart and pay you and then I'll drop you back."

I say, "You don't have to do that." But I have nothing else to do and I want a look at the house. We'd talked about this house. I found out he'd rented the house for $45,000 a month. He says, "I'll show you the house if you've got a moment and I want to pay you."

I say, "Sure." It's right across the street.

So we jump on this golf cart. He had a big bottle of water on it. He's drinking it. We pull up to this beautiful house.

I'm like, "This is pretty cool."

He's like, "Let me show you around." We were there about 15 minutes. It was a gorgeous house with a pool.

His wife comes out. I expect a super model, but she's the same age he is, maybe in her 50s. She says, "Would you like to have a drink, sweetheart?"

I say, "No, I've still got to work for the rest of the day."

She says, "Well, what if I give you a bottle of water?"

I say, "Sure."

I take the bottle of water and I'm thinking, Okay, guys, give me the money. Let's get the fuck out of here.

They're looking at each other and she says, "Why is he here?"

The guy says, "Oh, yeah, I forgot

to tell you. He's such a cool guy, I started showing him the house."

She says, "My husband does this all the time. I can't believe this."

He says, "Why don't you go into the garage, Oscar? I'm gonna make myself a drink. There's a bag there. There's some money in it. Take as much as you need."

I say, "Excuse me?"

He says, "Go in the garage. There's a bag. Like a Louis Vuitton bag. There's money in it. Take as much as you need."

I say, "Excuse me, sir. I can't do that. You gotta give me the money."

His manner changed immediately. He says, "What's the fuckin' big deal? When I tell you to do something, you go ahead and do it!"

I'm thinking, I'm in this house full of freaks. Are they gonna shoot me or keep me prisoner or what? People know I left with this guy, but they don't know where I went.

He says, "Just fuckin' get the money."

I'm like, "Okay."

I go in there and there's a bag. Full of money! Four or five bundles of money. Big bills. I take a $100 bill and

I come out of the room holding the money by two ingers. I say, "You have any change on you?"

He says, "Of course I do."

He opens a drawer, it's full of fives and singles, and I'm like, This is the weirdest thing.

He counts the money and gives me thirty bucks. No tip! You'd expect a big tip from him.

He says to me, "I know I promised that I'd drive you back, but I don't feel like it. I'm having a drink. Do you mind taking the golf cart and going back?"

I say, "Who'll bring it back?"

He says, "I don't know. We'll find somebody. Just take the golf cart and go back."

I say, "Seriously?"

He says, "Let me tell you something, kid. You gotta a fuckin' problem. When somebody tells you to do something, you just fuckin' do it. Why do you keep questioning me?"

I say, "Okay." So I take the golf cart, I go back to work and it gets picked up.

He comes a second day with the golf cart and he says, "Hey, Oscar, how are you doing today?"

I say, "Good. How are you doing?"

He says, "I want to come back for another shave and a haircut before we leave. I really enjoyed it."

I say, "Absolutely."

So he comes in and he has money but he had the money in that bag. The same bag. He opens it and takes out a $100 bill and says, "I assume you have change."

I look at him like, Is he fuckin' with me?

"Of course I do," I say.

I open my drawer and I give him the money. No tip. Off he went.

The Free Advice

This guy has long black hair. His name is Terry. He comes in and says, "Good morning, Oscar. How are you doing?"

I say, "Good. Can I help you?"

He says, "Can I sit down and you can tell me how I should have my hair cut? Can I get a consultation?"

I say, "Sure. Sit down." For five minutes we talk about his hair. He asks: Should I cut this? Should I do that?

I realize he doesn't really know and can't decide. I say, "Okay, dude. We can cut it short or long. You decide. When you're ready for the haircut, I'll give you an extra ten minutes for a consultation."

He says, "Thank you very much. I really appreciate it. Can I take your card so I can make an appointment? How much is a haircut?"

I tell him. He says, "Perfect! The price is great. I'm never gonna go anywhere else."

He comes in next week and says, "Oscar, can I talk to you about my hair for five minutes?"

I say, "Sure. Sit in my chair. What's the matter?"

Terry says, "Do you think I should use a regular conditioner? Should I use a hydrating conditioner? Or a volumizing conditioner? Or should I use a moisturizing conditioner? I got thick black hair down to my shoulders. I don't know if I should spend the money on hair products and make my hair better or spend the money on haircuts and get good haircuts."

I say, "You can do something in-between. You can get a haircut and you can use some different shampoos, something not too expensive."

He says, "Okay, can I make an appointment later? I'll take your card."

I say, "Okay."

So Terry picks my brain for a month, asking for my opinion. Then one morning, I see him passing by my shop. He has a short haircut. He waves at me.

I open the door and say, "Whoa, whoa, whoa, Terry. You gotta come inside. We're gonna talk about your hair."

He says, "Really? You wanna talk about my hair?"

I say, "Oh, yeah, I wanna talk about your hair. Sit in my chair."

He sits down and I say, "Terry! What the hell happened here? You came and bothered me for four weeks in a row, asking me what should we do with your hair: Should we cut it? If we cut it, how will we cut it?

"Then you get a haircut. Exactly the same cut I told you to get. Why didn't you get it here?"

He says, "Well, you weren't open."

I say, "You had my business card. You said, 'I will make an appointment.' You said the price was good. I spent a lot of time with you. How could you go somewhere else?"

He says, "I thought about it for a while before I went another place to get a haircut. I was talking to you and then I was talking to another stylist. And I was telling him everything you told me like I knew it and he kept agreeing with me. He kept saying, 'Yup, yup. You're very knowledgeable about hair. You know what you're talking about. I think that haircut would be great on you.' And he said he'd do it for half the price that you would do it."

I say, "Terry. That's not cool at all. How could you do that?"

He says, "I know. I know. It's a personality problem. I have to own it. I apologize."

I say, "You come here for a month, pick my brain, and then you go down the street and get the same thing for half the price!"

He says, "Yes."

I say, "You're gonna leave this shop and you're never coming back again. This is so unethical. I've never had a customer like you."

He says, "Okay."

Next year, during the season, here comes Terry again. He says, "Oscar! How are you doing?"

I say, "Terry! I still remember what you did. Don't treat me like I'm an idiot."

He says, "Do you really remember?"

I say, "Yes, I do."

He says, "I thought you would forget about it by now. You're very professional. You pay attention to what you do."

I say, "Get the fuck out of here." He leaves.

Next season, he comes in again.

He says, "Hey, how are you doing? I wanna get a haircut."

I say, "Terry, get the fuck out of here."

He says, "You still remember, huh? You're still angry?"

I say, "Yes, I am. Get the fuck out."

I moved to two more shops. Believe it or not, Terry followed me. This past season he comes in and says, "Hey, how you doing? I'm thinking of getting a haircut."

It's been ten years now. Every season he comes in and every season I throw him out.

The Dead Man's Hair

Have I ever done someone's hair when they're dead? Yes. I was in Canada. My friend was from Canada and she went home to visit her family in this small town near the US border. I'm a dark guy from the Middle East. I'm gonna stand out in a town of 15,000.

When you do hair, it's so easy to meet people. So this guy in a bar says to me, "Hey, where are you from?"

I say, "I'm from Turkey. I cut hair back home in Florida. I have a friend, she's from this town."

He knew my friend and her family. I say, "What do you do?"

He says, "What I do is a little bit different. I'm a funeral director. I restore the bodies of dead people who get in terrible accidents – who lose eyes, limbs, have badly damaged faces. That's my specialty."

I say, "Hey, man. That's pretty cool. But don't you get scared?"

He says, "No, I don't get scared. I worked with my dad and now my son is working with me. I take pride in what I do. Half the person's face is gone, and I look at the person's picture and I start putting him together from it."

I say, "What do you do with the hair?"

He says, "That's the hardest part, trying to get the hair right."

I say, "I'm gonna be in town for seven or eight days. I wouldn't mind cutting the hair to have it as an experience."

He says, "Would you really?"

I say, "Yeah, I've got nothing to do but drink all day long."

He says, "Okay, come to my place tomorrow."

So I did. *Ding-dong. Ding-dong. Ding-dong. Ding-dong.* I'm ringing the bell. Three minutes later he comes upstairs, and says, "Hey, Oscar. I have this man. He was in a helicopter crash. I'm working on him. I will sew the wig to his head and if you want, you can cut the hair."

I say, "Yeah. How should I cut the hair?"

He says, "We have a picture. The family says this is what he looked like. You can cut it this way."

Inside, it's like in the horror movies. This guy has a regular funeral home upstairs. We go down 15 or 20

stairs. It's not steep. It's like a
basement. There's a long corridor and
at the end of this corridor there's a
metal bed. It's metal so he can wash
the person. Like an autopsy table.

So here's this naked guy on the
table and the first thing I look at is his
dick.

I think, Oh my God, he's got a
big dick.

I like stopped, and the funeral
guy says, "Come on, there's nothing to
be scared of."

The dead man's hair was burned
off in the accident. The funeral
director did all the reconstruction on
the face. He put some make-up on
him. He was about 40 and must have
been a good-looking man.

The funeral director says, "Let
me sew on the hair and then you can
do the haircut."

I say, "Why can't we just cut the
hair first and then put the wig on?"

He says, "No, no, I have to do it
this way."

I say, "How are we gonna cut the
hair on the back of the head?"

He says, "What do you mean?
You don't have to cut the back of the
head. You just go around the ears

while he's lying down."

I say, "Yeah, but it's not a really good haircut."

He says, "Who cares? He doesn't care. He'll look good in the coffin."

I say, "Man, at least give the guy a proper haircut."

He says, "What do you want to do?"

I say, "Maybe we can sit him up."

He says, "He's heavy. We might sit him up and he'll get stuck like that. We have to be careful."

I say, "I have an idea. Do you have a low chair?"

He says, "Yes."

So we pulled the body all the way to the edge of the table, so the head was over the edge. I put a towel over the top of the chair and I put the man's neck there.

The mortician says, "Oh, I never thought about that."

So I'm on the floor, doing my thing, clipping away, and he says, "Oscar, it doesn't really matter. Just cut the hair."

After I finished the haircut, he says, "Hey, would you like to come to see him at the funeral?"

I say, "No. I don't really need to

see him at the funeral."

He says, "I should pay you for this service."

I say, "Not really. I just did it for the experience."

He says, "How do you feel about it?"

I say, "I felt pretty good about it."

He says, "Exactly. That's the reason I stay in this industry. Otherwise, if someone passes away and the family can't see their loved one, there's no closure for them. I put these people together. You've cut that man's hair. His wife is always going to remember him in great shape.

"If you want to continue, you could make a lot of money, just doing the hair for funeral directors."

I say, "Considering I'm in Canada, I'm not allowed to work. This just a complimentary cut. An experience that I will keep for life."

The Good Example

I'm in the middle of a divorce, so here I am on the streets, sleeping in a car. I don't have $5 in my pocket. I'm driving this leased car and I'm sleeping in it in a Starbucks parking lot. I see this kid coming to the car and he's just so excited about the car.

He says, "Wow, look at that car!"

His mom says, "Don't touch the car."

I get out of the car and the kid says, "Oh, I love your car."

His mom says, "See, you want to grow up and be successful like him."

The Famous Athlete

It's a rainy afternoon, and I see this famous athlete running on the beach. Everybody knows his name. He's internationally famous. Even if you don't watch his sport, you'd know who he is. I'll call him Glitter Joe.

I knew the beach bartender and I say, "What's with him? Is he really a wild guy?"

The bartender says, "That's Glitter Joe, and he's a wild dude. One thing: He never pays his bills. Look out for him. He runs a tab and when it reaches a couple hundred bucks, we cut him off until he makes a payment."

I say, "That's kinda lame. All the money he makes."

Later, I'm cutting hair and this guy walks in. I'm like, Oh my God, that's Glitter Joe.

He says, "Yo! What's up?"

I say, "What's up with you?"

He's really intimidating. He's got huge hands and a nose ring. He's a big guy. And he's wired. I can tell by his eyes. He says, "Hey, I want to send my son here for a haircut. Can he just come any time?"

I say, "No, I work with appointments. But he can come this afternoon, toward the end of the day."

Glitter Joe says, "He'll come and get the haircut and then I'll pay you later."

I say, "I don't work that way." Hell with that, he's not going to pay me – he's gonna skip out on the haircut.

I say, "Why don't you guys come together and you pay for the haircut?"

He says, "Do you know who I am?"

I say, "I don't know who you are." I know who he is, but I don't want to say so.

He says, "I'll come with my son."

So he comes with his son, who is maybe 14-15 years old. Super-cool kid. I cut his hair, we talk. Glitter Joe never says a word. He sat in the back and read magazines. Some famous people, they prefer to do that. He came in through the back door. He sat behind a partition and nobody made a big scene.

I cut his son's hair and Glitter Joe's keys and sunglasses were on my station. I kinda put them away because he's a crazy dude. He might skip out on me.

When I'm finished with his son's hair, Glitter Joe says, "Okay, bro. Love you, man. I'll come back and get my hair cut and colored."

I say, "Sure."

He says, "How much is the cut?"

I say, "Thirty bucks" for the son's cut.

He starts patting his pockets and says, "Oh, shoot, man. I don't have any money on me."

I'm thinking, Oh, man, this is exactly what I was expecting.

At this time, the shop is closing and we're the last ones left. The front door is locked and there's nobody in the shop except the three of us: Glitter Joe, his son, and me. I'm wondering what's going to happen. This dude is famous, he's big, he could punch me. I don't get intimidated often, but this guy was intimidating me.

But I'm thinking, Nobody leaves without paying for a haircut. I'm Oscar the Barber.

I dropped his keys into my drawer at my station. He says, "I got no money."

I say, "Maybe you left it outside."

He says, "You sure?"

I say, "I don't know. Maybe you dropped it outside. Maybe you should go check your car."

So he goes outside. As soon as he's gone, I locked the door. I have his son. And I have his keys.

He turns around and says, "Yo! You fucking locked me out?"

I'm like, "Dude. I know you don't pay your bills."

He yells at me, "Fuck you!"

Glitter Joe is screaming at me. My door is covered with spit. I'm thinking, Should I call 911? I've got the car keys.

I say, "Dude, give me my fuckin' money."

He says, "Fuck you! You piece of shit." He's just going at me. He says, "You're never gonna get paid. I wasn't going to pay you anyway. Who do you think you are?"

He walks off.

Three minutes later he comes back and knocks on the door. "Hey, Oscar."

I say, "What?"

He says, "Hey, man. Did I leave my keys there?"

I say, "I don't think so."

His son says, "Yeah, Dad. You

came in with the keys."

Glitter Joe says, "Look at your station."

So I do. I say, "Oh, I've got your keys."

He says, "Hey man, open the fuckin' door. Give me my keys."

I say, "Where's my money?"

He says, "Give me my fuckin' keys or I'm gonna call the fuckin' cops!"

I say, "Dude, you go call the cops. I'll tell them you didn't pay for a haircut. Until you give me my money, I'm not giving you these keys."

He was outside, screaming, my neighbors are outside. My next-door neighbor says, "I'll fuckin' pay for his fuckin' haircut."

They're taking pictures. He's crazy. One guy says, "Can we take your picture?"

Glitter Joe says, "Okay, bro. One picture."

Everybody is shouting, Glitter Joe is threatening me. There's a lot of noise. I'm sure someone's gonna call 911.

Finally, Glitter Joe says to me, "Man, you fuckin' got me." He takes out his money and says, "How much is a haircut?"

I told him $30.

He slipped the money underneath the door for me. No tip. He says, "Now give me my keys."

I say, "Dude, I'm scared of you."

He says, "I'm not going to do anything."

I say, "I'm scared. You need to back off. I'll throw out your keys."

So he backs off. I take his keys and I throw them out. He picks them up and he takes off with his son.

After that, I see Glitter Joe at a restaurant. A nice neighborhood place. I'm sitting at the bar. I know the bartender very well. He says to me, "Oh, shoot. We got trouble."

I say, "What's going on?"

He says, "Look who's coming." The bartender doesn't know what happened with Glitter Joe and me. Coming in is Glitter Joe. He's got three girls with him and he's drunk out of his mind.

I'm thinking, Oh, my God, he's gonna punch me.

I say to the bartender, "Give me my check. I'm outta here."

The bartender says, "Why?"

I say, "Don't ask me any

questions. I'm fuckin' outta here."

Glitter Joe sits next to me at the bar. He's looking at me. He says, "Hey, man, how are you doing?"

I say, "Good."

He says, "Bro, I know you from somewhere."

I'm like, "No. I never met you."

He says, "You know who I am, right?"

I say, "Oh, yes. You're famous."

He says, "I always remember a face. I know you from somewhere."

I say, "Oh, no. I need to leave."

He holds my shoulders and says, "No, no, we're gonna do shots together."

He yells, "Fuckin' shots on the house."

I'm saying, "I've got to go." I'm thinking, I can start a fight, or just do the shot and leave. My heart is pounding.

The bartender says, "Here are the shots."

I drink my shot so quick and say, "Okay, I gotta go. Have a good day."

I was outta there.

The Man Who Found a New Reason to Live

This pro football player called me and says, "Hey, is this Oscar the Barber?"

I say, "Yeah."

He says, "Do you do appointments or walk-ins?"

I say, "Most of the time, I take appointments. Sometimes I take walk-ins."

He says, "Great! I'd like to make an appointment. How big is your chair?"

I say, "It's big."

He says, "I'm a big guy and if it's a little tiny stylist's chair, it's not gonna work for me."

I say, "I have a big, heavy, thousand-dollar barber's chair."

He says, "That's great. Perfect. I'm a big, masculine dude."

He comes in and he's big. He's a big, good old boy. White dude. Shaved head. He wanted a flattop. I'm thinking, This chair is barely going to hold him.

When he comes in, he says, "Oscar, nice to meet you. I'm a

professional football player and I have a back problem. It spasms so much after I sit for a while that I have to lie down."

I say, "Okay."

He says, "Do you mind if during the haircut if I get up and lie down on your floor?"

I say, "No." What am I supposed to say? No, you can't?

So I start cutting hair and he says, "Ohhhh! Stop!"

He says, "I gotta lie down. I gotta lie down. I gotta lie down."

I say, "Okay."

So he gets out of the chair and literally lies down on the floor. He says, "I just need three minutes. I just need three minutes."

So everyone in the shop is looking at me like, What the hell is going on? I'm trying to pretend that everything is okay. I'm asking the football player, "You want any water?"

He says, "No, I'm okay."

So he gets up and I say, "How are you feeling?" and he says, "Much better. Thank you very much."

So he sits in my chair and I cut one side of his hair. He told me his pain was caused by an old injury. He was in a grocery store reaching for a bag, and . . . He starts yelling again, "Whoa, whoa, whoa! I gotta get up."

I'm thinking, This is going to be a long-ass haircut. We're like three minutes into it. He says, "Do you mind?"

I'm like, "No, no, go ahead."

He lies down on the floor. I say, "Are you okay?"

He says, "Oh, yeah. I just need three minutes."

He gets up again and I'm thinking, Oh, my God, what did I get myself into?

So we do the haircut with him getting on the floor every couple of minutes.

He gets back up and he says, "Oscar, thank you very much."

I'm thinking I should cut his hair while he's standing up, but he's such a tall guy, Do I get on a ladder to cut his hair?

He goes out to his car. He was literally lying down inside of his car. He was really in pain.

He comes in one time and he says, "Oh, I'm so excited. I'm gonna get these shots and my back is gonna be fixed. I hope everything works out.

I wanna play next season."

I'm thinking, Dude, you can't even get a haircut. What makes you think you can play football next season?

Again, he's screaming in pain and on the floor for three minutes, then back in the chair. Again and again.

He comes back the third time for a cut. He's so upset. I could tell. He's in pain and down on the floor. I say, "Dude, are you okay?'

He says, "Not really." And he started crying. He just broke down, lying on the floor. I'm thinking, This is so sad. He's crying, "I'm never gonna make it to the season. It's never gonna happen for me."

I'm like, "Dude, don't do that." Big dude on the floor, rolling around crying. My heart bled for him. He was like a big, gentle teddy bear.

I tell him, "Dude, things will get better." I'm trying to make him feel better and he's saying, "I never shoulda reached for that bag in the grocery store."

I say, "Things will get better and you will always find a purpose to live. If it's not football, it will be something else."

He says, "You're right."

He comes for a haircut several months later. I haven't heard from him during that time. He was still having back pain, but he got some injections and it wasn't as bad.

I say, "What's going on? Obviously, you're not playing football."

He says, "Yeah. Oscar, remember you told me that I would have another purpose in life? I found it. I found that purpose."

I say, "What is it?"

He says, "I'm playing tennis with Nintendo Wii. It's changed my life."

I say, "Are you fuckin' with me?"

He says, "Nothing gives me more pleasure than lying in my bed, moving my arms, playing tennis with my Nintendo Wii."

I say, "You found your purpose. Good for you."

The Abused Man

You always hear about women being abused by their men. Most people think that a man being abused by a woman is bullshit, because a man can beat her up – he can fight back, right?

I'd just taken my continuing education course on barbering and one of the chapters was how we should handle abuse if a client comes to us and says, "I'm being abused by my partner." I thought it was interesting that the people in the Florida government who regulate barbering and cosmetology saw that as a huge problem. Jim and his son, Dan, were both clients. Dan had this girlfriend I'd never met, but he talked very highly about her.

One day, I was joking around and tapped him on the shoulder.

He says, "Ow, dude, take it easy."

I say, "Why? What happened?'

He says, "You wanna see something crazy?" He opened the side of his shirt and the skin was pitch-black. Like someone had dyed it.

I say, "Dude! What happened?

Were you in a car accident?"

He says, "Oh, no. My girlfriend and I got into a fight. She hit me."

I say, "That's a big bruise. Does your girlfriend weigh 500 pounds?"

He says, "Oh, no, she's a very little girl. She weighs maybe a hundred pounds, but she hits me with whatever she has in her hand."

I say, "Dude, this is not normal. You gotta do something about this."

He says, "Well, we're working on it. We were both drunk. We shouldn't have been drinking."

I say, "Drunk or not, this is not normal."

He says, "I don't know. My dad says the same thing."

I say, "Listen to your dad. Get out of her way."

Dan kept coming to me, time after time. He was a cool guy. Young, in his 30s. His father was cool, too. I say to his father, "You've got to do something about Dan. He's being abused by his girlfriend – like physically."

His father says, "I know. We're trying to do the best we can. I don't know why he doesn't want to let her go. They shouldn't be living together."

Dan comes in another time and his stomach was completely black. She'd hit him again. Then one day, he didn't show up for his appointment, and that's not like him. We were really tight. He would have texted me if he couldn't make it.

Dan's father calls me and says, "Oscar, I've got bad news for you."

I say, "What happened, Jim?"

He says, "We lost Dan."

I say, "Oh, no. What do you mean?"

Jim says, "I can't talk. It's too hard for me."

I say, "No problem. Just text me about the funeral and I'll be there."

This story touches me very deeply. I was personally going through some stuff myself.

The funeral was in a church. I walked into a room in the church and there were maybe 20 people. Here's a guy in his 30s and there's only 20 people. He had nobody there. He'd always found excuses for his girlfriend: "She's just drunk. She's upset. It's gonna be better."

I looked at his parents and I saw their anger and sadness, all bundled up together. They didn't know what to say or what to do. But they were strong.

The girlfriend was there, too. Dan died from internal bleeding. But there was no evidence that she killed him.

They had a poem at the funeral. It said the only thing you leave behind is your legacy. The poem was very powerful. It said, "Try to leave a good legacy. If at least one person other than your parents says, 'I really miss him' – that's a legacy. When people truly miss you, that means you've brought something into their lives."

Dan changed the way I look at life. I'm a better person because of him. And I feel his absence.

The Man Who Sexted

I have this client, he never calls. He always sends text messages to make an appointment. He'll text me, "Hey, Oscar, how's tomorrow about 3 o'clock for a haircut?"

I'll text him back, "Great, Ted."

Later that night, he sends me some very sexual text messages. They say, "I would love to tickle your tonsils." Imagine getting a text message like that from your client.

I'm like, Oh, my God. I think this is the wrong text message. I text back, "Ted, this is Oscar. You're making a mistake."

He texts, "I never make mistakes."

I text, "This is weird, dude. Stop texting me. I'll see you tomorrow."

I show the message to him when he comes for his haircut and say, "Ted, you sent me this fuckin' text message."

He says, "Oh, my God, Oscar! I apologize so much. It wasn't intended for you. I have a friend, his name is Oscar, too. I don't know what to say."

I say, "It's okay. I tried to tell you this was Oscar and you said you never made mistakes."

Ted says, "I am deeply sorry. I apologize."

I say, "Okay, no problem."

Next month, he sends me another text, "Hey, Oscar. I want to come for a haircut."

I text him, "Sure. How about tomorrow at 2?"

I tell Helene, "I'm going to get a sexual text from him tonight."

Sure enough, his text says, "Hey, Oscar, I'd love to get a rubdown from you. I know you want it, too."

I text him, "Dude, this is Oscar the Barber. Stop this!"

He texts me, "Oh, my God. I apologize."

Month after month, he sends me these sexy text messages. Every haircut.

One day, he comes in and I say, "Dude, I have to ask you something."

He says, "What is it?"

I say, "I want to meet this Oscar. I don't believe he exists. I think you're sending me these texts just to get a reaction from me."

He says, "Okay. Let me set it up. There's a real Oscar."

We meet the other Oscar at a restaurant. Nice guy. Very good-looking guy.

Ted says, "See? This is Oscar."

He says to me, "Oscar, do you know how many times this fuckin' idiot asked me for a haircut? I kept telling him, 'You got the wrong guy!'"

I said, "Do you know how much times he asked me to tickle his tonsils? And I told him the same thing."

The Man Who Wanted Short Hair

In the salon where I used to work, I was the only guy who did men's haircuts. This man comes into the shop and says, "Hey, can I speak to the barber?"

The receptionist says, "He's in the back."

He comes in the back and I'm doing somebody's haircut. This man is very well-dressed. He says to me, "Excuse me, sir. I got a haircut here the other day. A young guy cut my hair. I don't think he cut it short enough. Would you be able to shorten it?"

I say, "A young guy. What did he look like?"

The man says, "Oh, a Spanish-looking guy."

I say, "Do you remember his name?"

He says, "No."

I say, "Well, I'm the only guy who cuts hair here. Nobody else would cut it except me. And I didn't cut your hair."

He says, "You know what? I apologize. I'm in the wrong place."

He apologizes again and leaves.

Next day. Same guy. Goes in the front. Wants to speak to the barber. He comes all the way to the back. I was cutting hair. He says, "Excuse me, sir."

I turn around. I'm like, "What?"

He says, "I got a haircut here the other day. There was a young guy, a Spanish-looking guy. He didn't cut it short enough. Would you cut it shorter?"

I say, "Are you kidding me? You were here yesterday. We talked to each other."

He says, "Oh, my God. You're right. I'm in the wrong shop again." So he goes out.

I'm thinking something is wrong with this man, maybe he's got Alzheimer's or something.

The third day, he comes in again. He says, "Excuse me, sir. I got a haircut here the other day. There was a young Spanish guy who cut my hair. But I don't think it's short enough."

I say, "Yes. Sit right there, sir. I will fix it immediately."

He says, "Thank you very much."

He sits down and says, "Can I have some coffee?"

I say, "Absolutely. Have some

coffee." I'm thinking, You son of a bitch, I'm gonna buzz you up so you'll never come back here again.

I say, "What was the name of the guy who cut your hair? Do you remember?"

He says, "No. He was a Spanish guy."

I say, "Where was he cutting hair?"

He says, "I don't know. It was in this shop. I'm certain it was here."

I say, "You want a short haircut, right?"

He says, "Yes."

I say, "Do you mind a clipper haircut?"

He says, "Oh, you seem to know what you're doing. I tell the guy who cuts my hair that he never takes enough."

I take my clippers and I buzz his hair. It's a crew cut. He was reading his magazine, not paying attention.

I say, "Is this short enough?"

His eyes pop for a second. Then he says, "Yes, I think it's pretty good."

Everyone in the salon is asking me, "What did you do?"

I say, "He got a free haircut, he'll never come back. Good."

The next day, I see him coming through the front door and I'm thinking, What now?

The manager comes back with the man. The guy says, "I got a haircut here the other day."

I say, "Yes, you did."

He says, "I have to be honest with you. It's a terrible haircut. You cut it too short."

I say, "What did the guy look like?"

He says, "He was a young, Spanish-looking guy." He's looking right at me.

I say, "You know what? He did so many bad haircuts, we had to fire him."

He says, "Did you really?"

I say, "Yes, it was very upsetting. He was such a nice guy."

He says, "Yes, he seemed like a very nice guy. Too bad. In that case, I'd like to get my money back."

I say, "Unfortunately, he wasn't an employee. He was renting a chair. I'm so sorry. If you want to come back later, here's my card."

He said, "You know what? You're a very nice professional man. I really appreciate the attention you gave me." And he left.

The Light at the End of the Tunnel

I get to meet a lot of people from the Northeast and Chad is one of them. He's got the *Godfather* theme as his ringtone. Very generous. I have met a lot of rich people, but I haven't met a lot of very giving ones. Chad goes to Haiti and builds an orphanage. His wife's birthday is the same day as mine. So every birthday, he comes in and gives me a hundred bucks. He'll say, "Hey, kid, do something."

He's so outgoing. A great guy. Great sense of humor. Athletic. White hair, slicked back. Beautiful wife. Mid to late 50s. He owns lots of businesses, including car dealerships.

Nothing can bring him down. Except one thing. His son, on a major birthday, gets a brand-new car from Chad. The son goes out partying with his friends, misses a curve, BOOM! – hits a tree and dies.

It's devastating to see death in somebody's eye. Chad will be getting his hair cut, we'll be talking, and something comes up – a car accident, or I'll make some stupid comment –

and the tears just come down his face. He's got a button that you just don't want to push there.

As the years go by, I got closer to him. He's got another son, a very cool guy who helps his father with his business. I met him.

He takes me out for dinner. We just talk light stuff. Maybe he sees the son that he lost in me. I've always felt that way. I look at him as the father that I would like to have. We've always had a connection.

When I was going through hard financial times, I was sleeping in my car and it was leased. I was so behind on the payments. I was having a hard time.

Chad heard about that and asked how I was doing. I say, "I'm going through very hard times."

He says, "Do you want money?"

I say, "No, no. I will not accept money unless I really need it. You know what I really need? A car. I just need a car."

He says, "You have no credit."

I say, "No."

He says, "You have no money."

I say, "No."

He says, "But you want a brand-new car."

I say, "It would be nice. I can try to make the monthly payments. I need something to get me going."

He says, "Send your application to my dealership. We'll see what we can do."

I take the application to the dealership and the guy says, "Kid. Are you kidding me? There's no way we can do this."

So I call Chad and I say, "Thank you very much, but it's just not possible. It's not gonna happen."

He says, "Oscar, don't give up so easy. You'll never get anywhere giving up so easily. I told you I would do it and I will get it done."

I say, "How are you gonna do it? The bank is not going to give me all this money to lease a car."

He says, "Let's see what I can do."

He calls me back in a week and says, "Where do you want me to ship the car?"

I say, "Ship the car!"

He says, "Give me an address. I got stuff to do."

I give him an address. He says, "Do you have the money for the

shipping?"
I say, "Uh. I'm not sure."

He says, "Okay, I'll ship the car down there with my cars." He ships this SUV.

That car was white. I always looked at that car like the light at the end of the tunnel. It jump-started me. Chad made it happen and opened another chapter in my life.

A New Start from a Stranger

I'm going through a divorce and I'm sleeping in my car at a Starbucks. I don't have $5 to buy coffee. One day, I go past this barbershop in a strip mall and I knock on the door. I ask the owner, Terry, "Do you have a chair for rent?"

He says, "Let's talk about it. Who are you? What do you do?"

I say, "I'm Oscar the Barber. I cut hair down the street. I'm getting a divorce. I'm literally on the streets. I'm a good guy. I'm very hard-working. I have my own barber's chair. I have no money. But I have my cell phone. I will call my contacts and make money immediately."

He says, "Sure. We can always figure it out later."

So I start cutting hair there. And he's a guy who gave me a chance.

When I was in trouble, I called all my friends. Some said they were on vacation, they'd call me back later. They never did. Nobody called me back. I was on the streets. But this stranger – the only thing we had in common was that we cut hair – gave me a chance. If I can cut hair, then I

can make money. He gave me a shot.
I'm here today, because he gave me a
chance. I'm here today because Terry
took a chance on me. I thank him
every day for it.

The Man Who Told Wild Stories

My client, Vito, was old school, New York, Italian, a womanizer, he smoked, he'd say: "fuck this, fuck that. Forget about it. Listen to what I tell you." He used to tell me stories. Wild stories about running things up to Canada, things like that. I thought, Yeah, Vito. Sure, Vito. Of course, Vito. I didn't believe him.

I used to smoke cigarettes, he used to smoke all the time. He had a stroke. After his stroke, he slowed down. He'd get a haircut and hang out in front of the place.

So one day I'm outside smoking a cigarette with him and he's telling me another story, how his friend TJ and him used to go to the casinos. All of a sudden, this young guy is passing by the shop. He walks, passes us maybe 6-7 steps, and stops. He starts coming backward, and he looks at us. The guy has a very thick New York accent and he says, "Excuse me, sir, are you Vito?"

Vito says, "Yeah, kid. Who the fuck are you?"

The young guy says, "Oh, my

God. My father, he always talks about you. I grew up hearing your stories."

Vito says, "So?"

The young guy says, "I just wanted to shake your hand, to meet you in person. My father says you were so good to the neighborhood, you were like Robin Hood, you'd take money from the rich and give it to the poor. You used to clear the neighborhood of the drug dealers, beat them up. You had another friend – was it TJ? The guy's a legend."

I'm thinking, Holy shit! Everything Vito has told me is true.

Vito says, "You know what, kid? You know too much about me. Now, get the fuck out of my face."

I'm like, "Vito, just be nice to the guy."

The kid says, "You know what? My father says, 'If you ever run into that son of a bitch, he's gonna tell you to fuck off.' I can't believe it. I'm gonna call my Dad and tell him you said that."

After the kid left I say, "Oh my God, Vito. Everything you've been telling me is true."

He says, "Yeah, what do you think – I'm lying to you?"

The Man Who Lost 20 Years

Al has been coming to me for a long time. When I first met him, Al says, "Hey, can I get a haircut with you?"

I'm like, "Of course."

He doesn't have much hair. He sat down and says, "Do you think it's gonna take a long time to cut my hair?"

I'm like, "No, I'm pretty quick. I should be able to get you in and out of the chair in 10 minutes."

He says, "Well, that's fine. Before you start the haircut, can I take my medication?"

I say, "Sure, man. You want a glass of water?"

He says, "No, no. I have these severe headaches and there's only one way to cut them off. Hold on a second and I'll show you."

He takes out a couple of pills and puts them on my station. He crushes the pills and then he snorts them.

I say, "Wow, I've seen people take pills, but I've never had anyone snort pain pills on my station."

He says, "Well, if you knew what

happened to me, you wouldn't blame me for it."

I say, "I'm not blaming you. It's your life and your body. Do what you have to do."

Al started coming in once a month. He graduated from three different universities and has three master's degrees. He liked cycling and a car hit him as he was cycling on A1A. Al hit his head on the curb and he lost his memory. He was in his early 40s when he had the accident and he can only remember his life until he was in his 20s. He remembers the last 15 or 16 years, but all his adult knowledge, career information and degrees are missing.

When I first met him, he was in his 40s and he had a big gap of almost 20 years of no memories. Because of that, he lost his job, he didn't remember any of his bank accounts, investments, anything he had until his family helped him find out things.

Today, he lives with a guy. Al says he's straight but they're really good friends, but he's got feelings for him.

Every time I give him a haircut, he says, "Oscar, I only remember things until I'm 22. But you are the best barber I've ever had. Therefore, your haircut is priceless to me."

And he opens his wallet and whatever money he's got, and he tries to give to me: $200 or $300 for a haircut.

I tell him, "Hey, this is a lot of money."

He says, "No, I want you to have it."

I don't want to do that. It's against my principles. But he's very insistent. Every time he comes in, he empties his wallet. I take the appropriate amount for a haircut, and I keep the rest in my pocket. Later, I call his partner and ask him to come get the rest of the money.

I see Al every month. He tells me the exact same story, and we have exactly the same conversation. He may have severe brain damage, but he still knows the difference between a good haircut and a bad haircut.

Barry and the Blind Man

Another man, Barry, has been coming to me for a long time, and he talked about his friend, Carl. Barry would say what a great guy Carl was, and they had all sort of plans. "Carl's gonna come down here when he retires," Barry would say. "His wife and my wife hang out together, we hang out together, we're very, very good friends. I've been talking about you and he's very excited to meet you."

I'd say, "Sure. I'd love to meet your best friend. I'll do my best as far as haircuts and anything else that goes with it."

So one day, Barry comes in and says, "Guess what? Next time I'm bringing in my friend, Carl."

I say, "Oh, that's great."

As soon as Carl walked into the shop, I knew something was off with him. Barry was holding his hand. I knew they were good friends, but I didn't think they had that much of a friendship – two old school guys from the East Coast, strong businessmen. I could see their friendship more than anything else by the way they held hands.

Very quickly, Barry says, "Carl gets a haircut first."

As soon as Carl sits in my chair, I saw he had long eyebrows. I say, "Do you want me to trim your eyebrows?"

Carl says, "Well, it doesn't make any difference. I don't see them anyhow."

I say, "You don't see them?"

He says, "Right. I don't see anything."

I say, "What do you mean? Barry has been talking about you and he was so excited to bring you down here to Florida. He had so many plans. He never mentioned that you were blind or had a disability – not that it would matter. I thought he would bring it up because he thinks so highly of you."

Carl says, "Oscar, my blindness wasn't part of the plan. I've had this eye degeneration problem for a long time, and I woke up Christmas morning with a total blackout. That was the day that I retired, and I haven't seen anything since that Christmas morning."

I say, "Wow, this must be very hard on you."

He says, "Yep. I did everything I

could, and things just didn't work out for me. However, I still like my Bloody Marys."

I look at this man and I say to myself, Wow, he is seeing something better than we see with our own eyes. This is a guy who worked his entire life, but he's never given up on life, or the pleasure he gets from it. It touched my heart.

Now every time Barry comes in, he gets a manicure, a haircut and a shave. And Carl gets manicure and a haircut. Today, Barry's wife and Carl's wife, they're all our clients. I call them, and they call me back.

One day Carl gives me his sunglasses to put away. I say, "Wow, man, these are really good sunglasses."

Carl says, "Do you really like them?"

I say, "Yeah, these are really cool. They fit you well."

Carl says, "Keep them."

I say, "I can't keep your sunglasses. They are very expensive."

He says, "Oh, it doesn't matter. Oscar, you've been so good to us."

I say, "Absolutely not. I cannot accept them. These are your glasses and they belong to you."

He says, "You got a point."

Next day, Barry shows up and gives me a brand-new pair of very, very expensive sunglasses. He says, "I want you to have these and I want you to keep these."

I say, "Thank you very much, but I can't accept this. This is a very expensive gift, and I was just making a comment about the sunglasses."

He says, "Oscar, I want you to keep them. My friend has no vision, but he saw you. Making me feel good and making my friend feel comfortable in your chair – the extra attention – that deserves an extra gift from us."

Eddie and the Strip Club CD

I used to go to a Dunkin' Donuts near my shop. Eddie was sitting with some of my favorite customers and they introduced us. Eddie started coming to me for haircuts. The first thing he asked was, "How much is a haircut?"

I was kinda surprised because the people he was hanging around with never questioned the price of a haircut. They were always so generous to me. I told Eddie the price and he found it expensive. I say, "I'm sorry, but that's the way it is."

He says, "That's okay, I'll get a haircut." He started coming to me on a spotty schedule: Every other month, or sometimes, he would skip a month or two and have longer hair.

I say, "Hey, Eddie, why don't you come for a haircut every three weeks? Obviously, you own a business."

He says, "Yeah, I own a business, but I don't think people care about my haircut that much."

I say, "Why?"

He says, "I own strip clubs."

I say, "Wow! You own the best

business ever. It must be hot and steamy and I'm sure customers and money are never an issue."

He laughs and says, "Yes, Oscar, you're right. I do have a great business. Sex sells no matter what. However, every time I go to work at night it's dark and I don't like to associate with my employees."

I say, "You mean strippers?"

He says, "Yes."

I say, "It doesn't matter. A haircut is a haircut and you should always pay attention to your grooming."

He laughs and says, "I have to be honest with you. I find this haircut very, very expensive. I can get the same haircut for half the price right down the street."

I say, "Really? I thought a haircut was something special and that we would have some communication with each other. You get a good haircut here. You're not sure what kind of haircut you're gonna get down the street. You might get a different person every time."

He says, "Yes, you have a point. I'm just being honest. I know you must be wondering, How come this guy never tips me? It's just the way I am. I got where I am by saving my money and watching out for it, and I never treat myself to expensive things."

I say, "It's your money. It's your place. You can do what you're gonna do."

Right after this conversation, a couple of my friends and I go to a bachelor party, so we ended up going to a strip club and had a great time. Two weeks later, Eddie comes into the shop with a CD in his hand.

He says, "You got time for a haircut?"

I say, "Of course, Eddie. I'll fit you in."

He's just sitting around, not saying much. I get the feeling he wants to say something to me but he doesn't know how.

I say, "What's going on?"

He says, "I'm gonna tip you today."

I say, "Whoa, what's going on? First, you find my haircuts expensive. Now you want to tip me today? Something must be up."

Eddie says, "The other day, I found out you were in one of my clubs."

I say, "I guess so. I went to a
bachelor party a couple of weeks ago."

He says, "I happened to be there
and I happened to video-record you
having a good time."

I'm like, "Oh, my God, how did
you do that?"

He says, "You guys were having
such a good time, I thought your
friend would want to remember it for
the rest of his life. Now I'm not
supposed to do that, and I'm not
supposed to give you a CD, and I'm
not supposed to record you guys at
all. But at the same time, I believe that
I'm not supposed to get expensive
haircuts or tip you. Sometimes, I do
things I'm not supposed to."

Mike the Gangster

It was a summer day and this blue-eyed, dark-haired good-looking guy walks into the shop. He looks at me with these piercing eyes and he says, "Can I get a haircut?"

I say, "Yes! It's a slow day. Sit your ass down. I'll cut your hair."

He was from New York and I learned to talk to New Yorkers like New Yorkers. They are not yelling at you. They are just talking to you.

As soon as he sits in the chair I say, "How do you want the haircut?"

He says, "Trim the sides and take a little bit off the top. I hear you're good. Do your thing."

I say, "Great."

So then he asks me, "Hey, do you know who I am?"

I say, "I have no idea."

He says, "I'll give you a head's up. What if I tell you my first name is Michael?"

I say, "Michael. Okay, Michael, I still don't know who you are."

He says, "Do you read any newspapers?"

I say, "Not really. I have to be honest. Maybe I glance at them."

He says, "Do you read the *New York Post*?"

I say, "Not really."

He says, "That's funny. I was passing by your shop and peeked inside your window. I saw a *New York Post* sitting on a chair in your waiting area and I thought that you might be reading it."

I say, "I do have customers who come in with that paper. When they leave, they say, 'Hey, I've read it. I'll just leave it around' and other customers read it while they wait. But I don't buy it."

He says, "That's interesting. I thought you read the *Post*. That's why I came in to get a haircut."

I'm like, "Michael, who are you?"

He says, "My name is Michael Soprano." That's not his real name, but I feel safer using it.

I say, "Okay."

He says, "Let me show you something." He takes out his own *New York Post* and opens the middle page and there's his picture with his father.

I look at it and I'm like, "Okay."

He says, "Now you know me."

I say, "You are being indicted and may go to jail?"

He says, "Yeah, but these fuckin' feds, they follow me everywhere. I can't get rid of them. Everybody knows me now. Everybody looks at me and points at me on the street. 'This is Michael. This is the guy. This is the gangster from New York.'"

I'm like, "Oookay."

He says, "As a matter of fact, they're even down here. The FBI is watching us."

I'm like, "What do you mean?"

He says, "They are right outside of your shop. In a Crown Victoria with tinted windows."

I say, "No way."

He says, "I am telling you."

I'm like, "Dude, I don't want to get myself in trouble."

He says, "Hey, how would you get in trouble? These fuckers have been following me all over the place, and when I meet people, I let them know that I'm supposed to be this big gangster and this FBI car has been following me."

I say, "Seriously? I don't believe that."

He says, "Walk out with me after you finish my haircut."

I say, "Okay, I'll fuckin' walk out

with you."

So we both walk out of the shop and sure enough, 200 feet away, there was one white Crown Victoria. It's got a US Government tag, and I'm like, No fuckin' way. This guy is telling me the truth. And if he is – why is he telling me this stuff?

He's saying, "Walk with me. Walk with me."

I'm like, "No, man. I don't want anything to do with this."

He says, "Watch me, then."

He goes to the Crown Vic and he knocks on the window very hard. The window rolls down and he says, "I FUCKIN' GOT YOU!"

Dino's Heart

Dino. Dino is a very famous restaurateur in town. He is a very demanding person. He will tell you exactly what he wants you to do and he will not hear anything else.

I was leaving work on a Saturday. I don't work Sunday and Monday. I get a phone call at 4:50-5 p.m. and I see it's Dino. He says, "Oscar, I'm in Naples" – the town on the west coast of Florida, not the one in Italy – "and I'm leaving here. I should be in Fort Lauderdale at approximately 7:30-8 p.m. tonight and I want to meet you at the shop to cut my hair."

I say, "Dino, it's Saturday, I'm finishing my shift, and I have plans with friends. I'm gonna go out and have dinner. I have to be honest. I will not come here to cut your hair at 8 p.m. on a Saturday night."

He says, "I'm telling you, you're gonna do it. I can get there a little earlier, like 7:30. If you stop talking on the phone I can get there even sooner. I'll call you when I get in town."

I say, "Dino! You're not hearing what I'm telling you. It's Saturday. I have plans with friends."

He says, "I'm going to have surgery Monday morning and I need to get this haircut."

I say, "Surgery? Are you okay? What's going on?"

He says, "God dammit, I'm not okay! I went to see my doctor and he says I need immediate open heart surgery. It's very urgent."

I say, "Dino, if you are getting open heart surgery, your haircut should be the least of your worries."

He says, "Well, don't you worry about my worries, I am worried about my haircut. If you'll get off the phone, I can meet you at the shop right before 8 p.m."

He was very angry with me. I told him, "I can understand that you are agitated, you're nervous, but I really have plans. I feel deeply sorry about what's happening to you, but I don't think this haircut will change the outcome of anything."

He hangs up the phone and I kinda feel bad that I didn't cut his hair.

I hear from him two weeks later. He says, "Hey, Oscar, are you in the shop?"

I say, "Yes, I am, Dino. How are you doing? How was your surgery?"

He says, "I can't talk much, but I'm going to give the phone to my wife."

His wife is such a lovely lady. She says, "Oscar, I know Dino can be a jerk, but would you take him back?"

I say, "Of course. I never barred him. I thought he would never call me back, knowing the way he is."

She says, "If you could cut his hair, we are right outside in the car."

I say, "I'll come out and help you guys into the shop."

She says, "That would be great."

So I go outside. They have a big Mercedes and Dino – two weeks after his surgery – is lying in the backseat.

He says, "You gonna cut my hair?"

I say, "Yes, Dino. I will cut your hair."

He says, "Pull me out by my feet, I don't bend so easy after the surgery."

I'm thinking, Why the hell do you want this haircut so bad? All he needs is a little trim.

I pull Dino out by his legs. It takes us ten minutes to get into the shop. He doesn't say anything to me at all. He has never tipped me.

At this end of this haircut, he says, "How much is the price?"

I tell him the price.

He says, "Damn, you're still so expensive." He pays and gives me half the amount of the haircut as a tip. He walks toward the door and says, "Thank you."

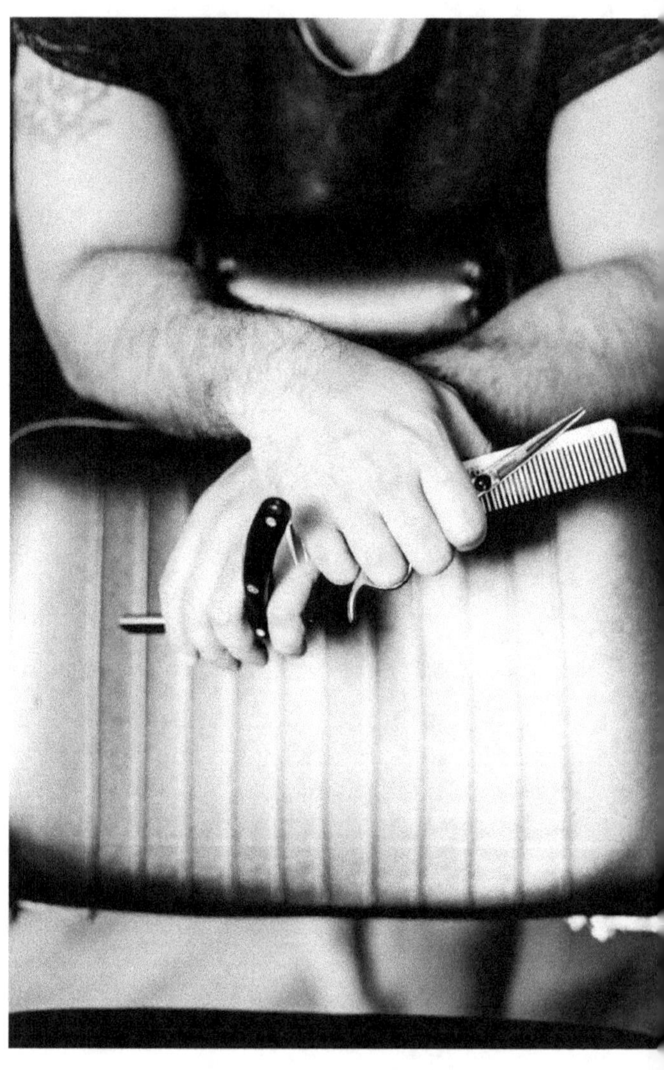

Contact Information
for Oscar the Barber

Oscarthebarber@yahoo.com

**Follow me on Instagram -
@__oscarthebarber__**

NOTES:

www.ingramcontent.com/pod-product-compliance
Lightning Source LLC
Chambersburg PA
CBHW061750250726
48657CB00001B/64